Figuring out the appropriate relationship between politics and religion for Christians is a daunting task. Yet Michael Gerson and Peter Wehner have succeeded brilliantly. In *City of Man*, they spell out a political theology for 21st-century Christians that rejects the narrow thinking of the religious right and the creeping secularism of the religious left. *City of Man* is a two-fer. It's an enormously important book on politics and on religion.

> —FRED BARNES
> Executive Editor, the *Weekly Standard*

Michael Gerson and Peter Wehner issue a clarion call for active Christian involvement in the form of calculated and thoughtful engagement. Chock-full of historical and theological wisdom, *City of Man* reminds Christians that they should care about politics and—win or lose—never give up the fights that matter most.

> —WILLIAM J. BENNETT
> Washington Fellow, the Claremont Institute

In *City of Man*, two of our nation's most gifted public intellectuals address the question, How should religious believers understand their obligations as citizens of a modern constitutional democratic republic? Addressing a range of challenging and timely issues, Michael Gerson and Peter Wehner show how the resources of Christian faith can be marshaled to bring public policy more fully in line with the inherent dignity of human beings, as creatures fashioned in the very image and likeness of God.

> —ROBERT P. GEORGE
> McCormick Professor of Jurisprudence and Director
> of the James Madison Program in American Ideals and
> Institutions Princeton University

Michael Gerson and Peter Wehner write out of both a rich experience in the national political arena and a deep immersion in biblical faith, and have given us a book of uncommon wisdom. Their reflections on how religion and politics interact in our rapidly changing culture are perceptive and challenging, combining a broad, historical understanding of the issues with a thoroughly accessible style.

> —STEPHEN A. HAYNER
> President, Columbia Theological Seminary

This book is a wonderful gift to all of us who care deeply about Christian engagement in the political arena. Drawing on their experiences of having worked day-to-day in the inner corridors of political power during times of crisis, the authors offer us a marvelously clear and candid perspective on what it means to seek the welfare of the "City of Man," while taking with utmost seriousness our identity as citizens of the kingdom of Jesus Christ.

—RICHARD J. MOUW
President, Fuller Theological Seminary

In recent American history, the mixture of religion and politics has all too often produced inflated rhetoric, demonization of opponents, runaway hyperbole, and mindless demagoguery. *City of Man* is different. It pulls back from the heat of conflict to seek light from Scripture, Christian tradition, and a measured analysis of American political history. Although I have voted "none of the above" in many presidential elections, I'm confident that what these veterans of the Bush White House have written will help Christian believers of any political persuasion to act more responsibly in the public square.

—MARK A. NOLL
Francis A. McAnaney Professor of History
University of Notre Dame

A thoughtful, creative articulation of a new agenda for conservative politics by Christians. One need not agree with all the assumptions or arguments to find this book a significant contribution to Christian reflection on where our nation should go. *City of Man* offers a significant challenge to both liberals and conservatives.

—RONALD J. SIDER
Professor of Theology, Holistic Ministry, and
Public Policy Palmer Theological Seminary

City of Man

**RELIGION AND POLITICS
IN A NEW ERA**

Michael Gerson
Peter Wehner

FOREWORD BY TIMOTHY KELLER

MOODY PUBLISHERS
CHICAGO

All Scripture quotations, unless otherwise indicated, are taken from the *Holy Bible, New International Version*®, NIV®. Copyright © 1973, 1978, 1984 by Biblica, Inc.™ Used by permission of Zondervan. All rights reserved worldwide.

Scripture quotations marked NJPS are taken from *Tanakh: The Holy Scriptures: The New JPS Translation according to the Traditional Hebrew Text.* Copyright 2000, The Jewish Publication Society. All rights reserved.

Scripture quotations marked NASB are taken from the *New American Standard Bible*®, Copyright © 1960, 1962, 1963, 1968, 1971, 1972, 1973, 1975, 1977, 1995 by The Lockman Foundation. Used by permission. (www.Lockman.org)

Scripture quotations marked ESV are taken from *The Holy Bible, English Standard Version.* Copyright © 2000, 2001 by Crossway Bibles, a division of Good News Publishers. Used by permission. All rights reserved.

All websites listed herein are accurate at the time of publication, but may change in the future or cease to exist. The listing of website references and resources does not imply publisher endorsement of the site's entire contents. Groups, corporations, and organizations are listed for informational purposes, and listing does not imply publisher endorsement of their activities.

Edited by Christopher Reese   Cover design: Faceout Studio
Interior design: Smartt Guys design   Cover image: Shutterstock 27472969

Library of Congress Cataloging-in-Publication Data

Gerson, Michael J.
    City of man : religion and politics in a new era / Michael J. Gerson and Peter Wehner ; foreword by Timothy J. Keller.
        p. cm.
    Includes bibliographical references.
    ISBN 978-0-8024-5857-5
    1. Religion and politics. 2. Religion and state. I. Wehner, Peter. II. Title.
BL65.P7G47 2010
261.7—dc22

                                        2010030107

We hope you enjoy this book from Moody Publishers. Our goal is to provide high-quality, thought-provoking books and products that connect truth to your real needs and challenges. For more information on other books and products written and produced from a biblical perspective, go to www.moodypublishers.com or write to:

Moody Publishers
820 N. LaSalle Boulevard
Chicago, IL 60610

1 3 5 7 9 10 8 6 4 2

Printed in the United States of America

To all the spiritual descendants of William Wilberforce
—Michael Gerson

To Cindy, John Paul, Christine, and David,
who have filled my life with so much joy,
so much love, and so many blessings
—Peter Wehner

Seek the welfare of the city to which I have exiled you, and pray to the Lord in its behalf, for in its prosperity you shall prosper.

Jeremiah 29:7 NJPS

Contents

A Cultural Renewal Series

GENERAL EDITORS:
TIMOTHY KELLER, COLLIN HANSEN

As an exercise in public theology, Moody Publishers' Cultural Renewal series brings biblical thought to bear on matters of contemporary concern. Resources for the church and by the church abound, yet a need remains for deep, sustained, faithful Christian reflection on pressing cultural questions. This series attempts to shape key conversations for the common good. Our challenges today—daunting and complex though they may be—do not intimidate the God who inspired the apostles and equipped great Christian leaders throughout history. By looking to their wisdom, humbly relying on God's provision of common grace and, especially, His Son, the church still has much to offer the world—now and always. *To God alone be the glory.*

Foreword

In the mid-twentieth-century, H. Richard Niebuhr wrote his classic *Christ and Culture*, which helped mainline Christian churches think through ways to relate faith to politics. In the end, Niebuhr came down on the side of universalism, the view that ultimately God is working to improve things through all kinds of religions and political movements. The result of his work was to lead mainline Protestant churches to become uncritical supporters of a liberal political agenda (though Niebuhr himself opposed such a move).

However, the mainline churches have shrunk and aged. Today, it is the more theologically conservative evangelical and Pentecostal churches that are growing, and they now outnumber mainline Protestants. Yet at the very same time, the number of secular Americans—those who claim not to believe in God, or at least to have "no religious preference"—are also fast rising in number.

This creates a far more complicated situation than the one that

Niebuhr faced over half a century ago. In today's society we have *both* rising secularism and rising orthodoxy. We have political polarization that would have been unimaginable a generation ago. And we have an evangelical constituency that is growing and institutionally powerful, but which is also culturally impotent. Why? It is largely because it has not done the hard work of thinking through the same issues that Niebuhr pondered decades ago. But it must do so now in a very different cultural and historical situation, and with a much greater trust in the ancient sources of orthodox theology and in the reliability of the Scriptures.

The present volume seeks to do this in one particular area, that of politics. My friends Michael Gerson and Pete Wehner are excellent guides. They write as political conservatives, but they begin with a critique of the Christian right. A very large number of young evangelicals believe that their churches have become as captured by the Right as mainline churches were captured by the Left. Michael and Pete recognize this and largely agree. But they counsel that political withdrawal is not the correct response, nor should alienated evangelicals go down the mainline path. Instead, they urge careful theological reflection, and the rest of this short volume serves as a guidebook to the issues that will have to be addressed, rather than as a finished manifesto of what this new political theology must be.

They begin by making critical distinctions between the roles of the believing individual, the institutional church, and the state. On this foundation, they introduce the issues of human rights, law and order, the role of the family, the nature of wealth and prosperity, and public discourse. In each case they define the field, show what religious believers can contribute, outline mistakes that have been made in the past, and finally hint about directions they would like to see believers take in the future. Evangelicals who are Democrats will probably wish the authors struck some additional notes or made some points differently, but overall this is a wonderfully balanced and warm invitation to believers of every persuasion to re-engage in political life, more thoughtfully than before, but as passionately as ever.

Some evangelicals will say that this is a distraction, that we should concentrate fully on the only important things—the defense of orthodox doctrine and the evangelism of the world. Yet, as the authors point out, in 1930s Germany, a faulty understanding of how Christianity relates to the political contributed to the disaster of Nazism, which in turn meant the loss of the German Lutheran Church's credibility, evangelistic witness, and even orthodoxy. Something similar happened in South Africa, where an orthodox Reformed theology, invoking the views of Abraham Kuyper, created a civil religion that supported apartheid, and as a consequence has suffered incalculable loss to its standing in the eyes of the people. Ironically, the Lutherans followed a two-kingdom approach to Christ and culture, in which Christians are not to bring their faith into politics, while Reformed Christianity has been characterized by a view that Christians are supposed to transform culture. Both approaches, when not applied thoughtfully and wisely, have led to cultural, political, and ultimately spiritual disaster.

What does this mean? It means that any simplistic Christian response to politics—the claim that we shouldn't be involved in politics, or that we should "take back our country for Jesus"—is inadequate. In each society, time, and place, the form of political involvement has to be worked out differently, with the utmost faithfulness to the Scripture, but also the greatest sensitivity to culture, time, and place. This book is a great beginning.

—Timothy Keller
Senior Pastor
Redeemer Presbyterian Church

Preface

Faith is among the most personal of matters. But political theology—a shorthand description for how people of faith view politics—has profound public consequences. And those consequences affect the religious and the non-religious alike.

In 1930s Germany, many Christians were influenced by a political theology that encouraged broad deference to the state; they also carried the baggage of a long, disturbing history of anti-Semitism. Whole denominations calling themselves "German Christians" quickly accommodated themselves to the rising Nazi ideology.

There were, of course, heroic exceptions. But they were exceptions. On the whole, the political theology of Christians in Germany was deeply discrediting to their faith. And this failure of conscience and courage had terrible consequences for Germans of other faiths and of no particular faith at all. A corrupted political theology helped lead to suffering beyond measure. The failure to confront Europe's genocide was one of the greatest scandals of religious history.

But now consider a very different example. Within a generation of these awful events in Europe, a movement of conscience, rooted in African-American churches, began to transform America for the better. The political theology of the civil rights movement, in stark contrast to that of German Christians, emphasized the equality of individuals rooted in the image of God, the power of redemptive suffering, and the biblical promise of liberation given to the Hebrews in Egyptian slavery.

Christian churches, in this case, became a place where people organized resistance to oppressive state governments and a refuge to those fleeing persecution. Even at the cost of suffering attacks and terrorism themselves, African-American churches along with their allies in mainline Christian denominations brought honor to the faith they held. More: their example of conscience motivated political changes—including the Civil Rights Act and the Voting Rights Act—that benefited untold numbers outside their own religious communities.

Complicity in genocide, the redemption of a nation's promise: two starkly opposed examples of the consequences that can flow from a political theology. One can offer many others. Clearly, the political views of influential religious groups can and do determine much about the shape of entire societies. In Saudi Arabia, Wahhabi Islam justifies a system of comprehensive oppression. In Burma, Buddhist monks have led the opposition against a cruel regime. In the United States, religious conservatives, who have taken a broader role in politics over the last few decades, have likewise influenced society, in ways we shall talk about in this book.

EVANGELICALS AND THE RELIGIOUS RIGHT

Fifty years ago, a serious discussion of political theology in America would have begun, and perhaps ended, with the views of the liberal religious mainline. Thinkers such as Reinhold Niebuhr shaped Protestant attitudes on social justice and war and peace. And these attitudes were broadly influential. Liberal Protestants took leadership roles in projects of social reform, and convened ecumenical discussions with Jews and Catholics.

But the mainline churches of fifty years ago are now "sideline churches," in the vivid words of the late Richard John Neuhaus. Liberal Protestant churches have undergone a dramatic decline in attendance and influence—in part because they became narrowly and predictably political. At the same time, conservative Protestant churches and movements have grown in relative influence. Protestants remain a majority in the United States, but a majority of this majority is now made up of the theologically conservative. According to the Pew Forum on Religion and Public Life, more than one-quarter of American adults belong to evangelical Protestant churches—more than belong to either Catholic or mainline Protestant churches.[1]

The term "evangelical Protestant" here includes both fundamentalists and evangelicals. These two groups share theologically conservative assumptions on the authority of the Bible and on the need for salvation through a personal decision to accept God's grace through Jesus Christ. But they tend to differ on the issue of social involvement. Traditionally, fundamentalists have been cultural separatists, believing that Christians should remain unsoiled examples in the midst of a hopelessly fallen world. Evangelicals are more oriented toward civic and cultural engagement, and more willing to work in common purpose with those who don't share their theological beliefs.

In recent decades, it is the evangelicals who have been ascendant. Richard Land, the president of the Southern Baptist Convention's Ethics and Religious Liberty Commission, estimates that his denomination—the largest Protestant denomination in America—includes 15 to 20 percent fundamentalists.[2] The rest, apart from a very small number of theologically liberal Southern Baptists, are evangelical.

Christians belonging to historically black churches—about 7 percent of American adults—tend to share the orthodox theological views of white evangelical Protestants. But their different history has given many African-American churches a different political theology.

In *City of Man*, we focus on the portion of the evangelical community that gave rise to the religious right. We do so for several reasons. The first is that, since the 1970s, the religious right has gained influence in American politics to the point where it now constitutes the most influential element of the Republican coalition and has become perhaps the single most influential religious community in the country. The beliefs of evangelicals have broad consequence.

In addition, the two of us are both evangelicals and political conservatives. The religious right is the movement we know the best and have dealt with the most closely. We share many of its concerns. On numerous issues of policy, we come down on the same side. Yet, as readers will discover, we are hardly uncritical. Our concerns take in matters of theological substance, and also of tone. James Madison said that all of us owe our country "loving criticism": an honest account and a candid assessment, undertaken with the aim of melioration. This is what we try to do here.

PRIVATE RELIGION

Surveying the checkered history of religious involvement in politics, many non-religious people throw up their hands in dismay. Everyone would be better off, they say, if religious people would just keep their views to themselves.

There is a long history here. Following Europe's bloody wars of religion, Enlightenment thinkers in England and on the Continent argued that the only safe option was the privatization of religion and its complete separation from the public realm. But the two historical examples we have considered above point to the limitations of this view. Christians in Germany should have been *more* public in confronting Nazi authorities. Americans have reason to be grateful that the leaders of the civil rights movement did *not* regard their faith as something fundamentally private. Besides, since the Enlightenment, more than one experiment in enforced privatization and/or complete secularization—the French Revolution, Leninism, Maoism—has ended in disaster for the causes of human rights and human dignity. There are dangers, it seems, both in societies dominated by religion and in societies where religion is banished.

WALKING THE TIGHTROPE

To the faithful, nations and governments are but temporary, while the journey of the soul is eternal. But it is in the public expression of their faith that we can discern the deepest commitments of the faithful. Do they concern themselves mainly with themselves, or with others? In their mode of life do they exemplify judgment, or grace? Is theirs an angry God, or a loving One? In the wake of the recent massive earthquake in Haiti—a tragedy extinguishing more than a quarter-of-a-million lives—many rushed to alleviate the suffering of the Haitian people; one prominent religious leader, however, asserted that the event was God's punishment on a nation that had made a pact with the devil. Both responses express a political theology: a view of how religious people should react to injustice in the world.

Sorting out the proper relationship between religion and politics is particularly difficult for Christians. Unlike Moses or Muhammad, Jesus of Nazareth did not set out a political blueprint or ideal of any kind. He specifically rejected the political utopianism of some of His followers. He lived within a Roman Empire whose existence He hardly mentioned. Jesus' main arguments were with religious authorities, not political ones. He proclaimed a kingdom "not of this world," a kingdom based not on an alternative leadership but on transformed lives.

Yet Jesus was executed as, in part, an enemy of the state. Contemporary leaders, political and religious, found His otherworldly kingdom threatening because it demanded obedience to an authority beyond their own. Jesus' followers were soon being executed for failing to show proper respect (that is, refusing to offer sacrifices) to the Roman emperor. In the Roman world, Christians challenged the political status quo on any number of issues, including slavery, infanticide, and the status of women. Christianity may not have laid out a blueprint for an ideal government, but "love your neighbor" had social and political consequences.

Christians in every generation have dealt with the same tension. They inhabit, in St. Augustine's vivid image, the City of Man—the flawed and fallen realm of history, government, and politics—while owing their ultimate allegiance to the City of God.

This dual citizenship is difficult. Historically, when the faithful have exercised political power, they have sometimes been responsible for oppression and have brought discredit on the faith itself. Christians have seldom been less appealing than when acting in the name of "Christendom." But when the faithful have ignored political power, they have sometimes again brought discredit on their ideals. Sins of omission can be as deadly as sins of commission. So the exercise of politics requires walking a tightrope. It is both a temptation and a responsibility; it can act like an addictive drug or a healing medicine.

Reflecting on these issues is always worthwhile. Today it is urgent. The reason is plain: we live in a time when our character-shaping institutions are weak, when sources of moral authority are in many respects on the defensive, and when the concept of truth itself often seems up for grabs.

We two do not share the concern of those who fear that America is about to enter a new Dark Age. That is far too sweeping and simplistic. But we do believe that an orderly, decent, and just society requires the cultivation of certain habits of the heart, a willingness to strive for moral excellence and defend moral truth. Such things are difficult to attain and easy to lose. And in America, the foundation and practice of such moral virtues has been inextricably tied to religious beliefs—in particular, to the vitality of Christian beliefs. "Of all the dispositions and habits which lead to political prosperity," George Washington famously said in his Farewell Address, "religion and morality are indispensable supports."

Those supports continue to be necessary today. People willing to strengthen those supports deserve to be encouraged. So, too, do those ready to speak out on behalf of virtue and the good life, on what is noble and is worthy to be valued. These are subjects about which people of faith ought to have a great deal to say.

A MOMENT OF TRANSITION

The faithful in America have entered a period of transition. One political theology—the model of the religious right—is passing. Another, still unformed, is taking its place. It is an exciting moment, when new movements and institutions are taking shape. It is also a precarious moment—a moment when apparently small flaws could eventually lead to large cracks, rendering the vessel useless. Errors at the beginning of an enterprise are always the most dangerous. A time of change is also a time of heightened responsibility.

The passing of the religious right is less a value judgment than a fact of life. The political theology that arose among politically conservative Christians in the 1970s was largely a defensive reaction to the aggressions of modern secular elites against traditional norms. These assaults—banning school prayer, attempting to regulate Christian schools, *Roe v. Wade*, among others—led conservative Christians to re-engage in American political life after a long period of cultural retreat. But the result was a narrow agenda and an often negative tone. The religious right became closely tied to the political party that was the less secular in its outlook—the GOP—and uncritically adopted many of its ideological habits. In the end, religious conservatives seemed to form just one more element of a political coalition controlled by others.

That model is changing, and quickly. Many white, evangelical Christians no longer wish to be identified with the tone and approach of the religious right. The generational shift from leaders such as Pat Robertson to leaders such as Rick Warren has been dramatic. A new cadre of evangelical political and cultural leaders is less interested in resisting the predominant culture than in shaping it. Evangelical activists are involved in an increasingly broader range of social concerns, including poverty, religious freedom, the environment, and world health. The American evangelical movement has become more global in orientation, more diverse in background, and less tied to a single political party.

Yet, even as all this is happening, many evangelicals are confused. They are uncomfortable with the image and conduct of the religious right, but, as biblical Christians, they remain morally conservative. They are also suspicious of the social gospel of liberal Protestantism, which often seemed to replace the biblical gospel with social activism. They sense that both the religious right and the religious left may be treading the same path—baptizing someone else's policy preferences and calling the result Christian. They wonder if there is a way to avoid repeating the same old mistakes in new ways.

Confusion is better than artificial certainty; but, as G. K. Chesterton said, "The object of opening the mind, as of opening the mouth, is to shut it again on something solid." In the realm of politics, some issues and causes are urgent. Suspending judgment is itself a kind of judgment: a vote for inaction. However difficult the challenge, it is also unavoidable. Like Jacob, we are required to wrestle with this angel.

A LOOK TO THE FUTURE

Our wrestling resulted in *City of Man*—a book addressed to religious people struggling to understand the relation of religion and politics, and to anyone interested in the form of engagement that conservative Christians might adopt in the future. In its pages, we hope to present a clear-eyed assessment of the religious right—its successes and its failures; to describe the searching and changes taking place among conservative Christians as they move beyond the religious right; and to draw out the implications of these shifts for American politics. But we also aim to begin the task of outlining a political theology for a *new* generation: a guide to thought and action for Christians in the political realm, and in the areas of both foreign and domestic policy. How *do* religious people exercise influence while maintaining their integrity? What tone *should* they be known for? Which causes and issues, at home or abroad, *ought to* be part of their agenda?

We are not theologians and do not pretend to be. We are former public officials who have wrestled with these issues in a thousand practical ways. We are political commentators who believe that the realm of ideas should inform the world of practical policy. And we are Christians whose faith is more important than our politics, and who know that religion should never be used as the means to serve narrow political ends. No book can serve two masters—both God and the party line. So we strive to address political issues without being partisan. It is, indeed, one of our main points that, just as a privatized faith can be irresponsible, a politicized faith is by definition less than faithful.

Ours is very much a book for now. A political theology is never written once for all, or for everyone. The duties of religious people in politics vary in different times and in different societies. Particular priorities and responsibilities will commend themselves to Christians living in constitutional monarchies, in totalitarian dictatorships, in representative democracies. Christianity has shown a remarkable ability to influence public life in a variety of settings.

But it is the duty of every generation to consider these issues in its own setting and by its own lights. Especially in a representative democracy, every citizen shares in the responsibility of governing; no one is merely a spectator. So what does it mean to be a Christian citizen in history's most influential nation; in a world marked by growing interconnection, danger, and need; in a time of bitter domestic polarization and economic stress?

How should we live, according to the best of our faith, in this City of Man?

NOTES

1. "U.S. Religious Landscape Survey: Summary of Key Findings," Pew Forum on Religion & Public Life, 2007, http://religions.pewforum.org/reports.

2. "God's Country? Evangelicals & U.S. Foreign Policy," Pew Research Center Publications, September 26, 2006, http://pewresearch.org/pubs/73/gods-country.

CHAPTER ONE

Religion and Politics: Friends or Enemies?

In the course of our common pilgrimage of faith, one of the many things we discover is that the Scriptures can be difficult to reconcile. At times, different verses and injunctions seem to make different claims and to demand different and sometimes even contradictory responses.

For example, Jesus tells us, "Blessed are the peacemakers, for they will be called sons of God." And yet, five chapters later in Matthew's gospel, Jesus says, "Do not suppose that I have come to bring peace to the earth. I did not come to bring peace, but a sword."

In the book of Romans we learn that "all have sinned and fall short of the glory of God," even as we are called to be perfect as our heavenly Father is perfect. The Hebrew Scriptures tell us to honor our fathers and mothers, and St. Paul instructs husbands to love their wives as Christ loved the church—yet Jesus declares, "If anyone comes to me and does not hate his father and mother, his wife and children, . . . he cannot be my disciple."

Are these and other verses truly irreconcilable? No; but reconciling them requires careful study and reflection. It can be dangerous, or even heretical, to build whole doctrines on a single verse without taking into account other verses and, especially, the historical context.

What is true about the Bible's prescriptions in general is true in particular for its teachings on Christian involvement in politics and governance. On one side we are told that Jesus is Lord of everything. According to the Christian account of things, God has never been detached from the affairs of this world; to the contrary, He has played an intimate role in its unfolding drama—from the creation, to the exodus of the Hebrew slaves from Egypt, to the incarnational presence of Jesus. God, the Bible teaches, is the author of history, and is not indifferent to the realm of politics and history.

So it would be foolish to exclude politics from the things over which God has authority, especially since civil government was itself established by God. Of the hundreds of prohibitions in the sixty-six books of the Bible, none is against people of faith serving in government.

We can put the point much more positively than that. In the Hebrew Bible, certain kings win the outright approval of God. In the New Testament, St. Paul argues that Christians should be good citizens and faithfully discharge their obligations to the state. Jesus Himself says we should render unto God the things that are God's and to Caesar the things that are Caesar's.

Still more positively, Christians should *care* about politics. The reason is that political acts have profound human consequences. It makes a very great difference whether people live in freedom or servitude; whether government promotes a culture of life or a culture of death; whether the state is a guardian or an enemy of human dignity. And whatever form of government we live under, we as individuals are enjoined to be mindful of our own civic duties. The prophet Micah tells us to do justice and to love mercy. We are called to oppose evil, to see to the needs of "the least of these," to comfort the afflicted, to feed the hungry, to help free the captives.

But doesn't the Bible also clearly teach that some things are far more *important* than politics? It does. Before the time of Jesus, it was expected that the Messiah would come as a political leader. Instead, He came as a lowly servant, born not to noble privilege but in a manger in Bethlehem. The disciples recruited by Jesus did not enjoy worldly status or influence. On a high mountain in the wilderness, Satan tempted Jesus by offering Him the kingdoms of the world and their glory. He declined, emphatically.

Jesus and His disciples also demonstrated a profound mistrust of power—especially political power. The focal point of Christ's ministry—the objects of most of His energies and affections—were the downtrodden, the social outcasts, the powerless. Regarding a Christian's place in the world, Jesus said, "My kingdom is not of this world." None of the disciples led anything approaching what we would consider a political movement, and all of us are urged to be "strangers and pilgrims" in the City of Man. Finally, there is Christianity's most sacred symbol, the cross—an emblem of agony and humiliation that is the antithesis of worldly power and victory.

History, especially the history of the church, may seem to offer its own reasons for demarcating Christianity from the sphere of politics. According to the social philosopher Jacques Ellul, every time the church has gotten into the political game, it has been drawn into self-betrayal or apostasy. "Politics is the Church's worst problem," Ellul wrote. "It is her constant temptation, the occasion of her greatest disasters, the trap continually set for her by the Prince of this World."[1]

Given these cross currents, it is little wonder that throughout history Christians have adopted fundamentally different, and even diametrically opposed, approaches to politics and governing.

The Anabaptist tradition—which grew out of the Reformation and now includes the Amish, Mennonites, and Plymouth Brethren movements—takes the view that Christian allegiance should be to the kingdom of God alone. If politics demands deep involvement in this world, holiness involves separation from it. For some Anabaptists, the duties of a Christian are restricted to praying for those in political authority, paying taxes, and passively obeying the civilian government. Others focus more on the example of the church itself as an alternative society. "The first task of Christian social ethics," writes Duke University's Stanley Hauerwas, "is not to make the 'world' better or more just, but to help Christian people form their community consistent with their conviction that the story of Christ is a truthful account of our existence."[2]

At the other end of the spectrum are figures who have wanted the church to govern earthly affairs, so as to bring society better into line with their understanding of God's will. This view goes back at least to the Roman Emperor Constantine, who in the fourth century first granted Christians freedom of worship, along with political privilege. Under his rule, Christian bishops functioned in an official political capacity, and the power of the state was used to enforce doctrine. In the course of a century or so, the position of Christians in Rome went "from the church against the state to the church for the state."[3]

Pope Innocent III, who lived in the thirteenth century, viewed himself not simply as a spiritual leader but as a temporal ruler—and he proved it by seizing authority away from the secular government. During his reign, the papacy was at the height of its power; it was, in effect, a theocratic superstate. In more recent times we have the model of the Church of England, the officially established church of the realm, and one that believes it has an affirmative duty to shape society. In fact, the bishops of the Anglican Church of England sit in the House of Lords, where they are called "the Lords Spiritual."

Between these two poles one finds thinkers such as Augustine, Luther, and Calvin, and, approaching our own times, Abraham Kuyper, Karl Barth, and Reinhold Niebuhr.

St. Augustine ranks as arguably the most influential Christian thinker after St. Paul, and his book *The City of God* may be the most influential Christian work of the Middle Ages. In addition to its many other significant achievements, this book created what has rightly been called a "theology of history."

It is to Augustine that we owe the concepts of the City of God and the City of Man—the former anchored in "heavenly hopes," the latter in "worldly possession." Tracing the history of these two cities, Augustine concludes that, ultimately, the City of God will triumph. Until then, however, we live in the City of Man, the result of the fall and of a defect in the human will.

For Augustine, the purpose of the state is to restrain evil and to advance justice, for, "in the absence of justice, what is sovereignty but organized brigandage?"[4] But such justice can only approach true—divine—justice insofar as it is informed by the "heavenly hopes" that flow from the City of God. As the theologian Robert E. Webber comments,

> [T]rue justice exists only in the society of God, and this will be truly fulfilled only after the Judgment. Nevertheless, while no society on earth can fully express this justice, the one that is more influenced by Christians and Christian teaching will more perfectly reflect a just society. For this reason, Christians have a duty toward government.[5]

Martin Luther (1483–1546) propounded a different vision: two kingdoms, one carnal and the other spiritual, each needing to remain separate from the other and each making its own legitimate demands. Still, Luther's views, while somewhat dualistic and quietist, did not advocate withdrawal from the world or preclude Christian participation in political affairs. We need both kingdoms, Luther maintained, "the one to produce righteousness, the other to bring about eternal peace and prevent evil deeds."[6]

To John Calvin (1509–1564), God was not only Lord and Creator but "a Governor and Preserver, . . . sustaining, cherishing, superintending all the things which He has made, to the very minutest, even to a sparrow."[7] The sovereignty of God, in other words, extends to *all* spheres, including all human institutions. The active purpose of the state, Calvin wrote, is "to foster and maintain the external worship of God, to defend sound doctrine and the condition of the church, to adapt our conduct to human society, to form our manners to civil justice, to reconcile us to each other, to cherish common peace and tranquility." Beyond providing merely for peace and safety, civil authorities, according to Calvin, are the "ordained guardians and vindicators of public innocence, modesty, honor, and tranquility."[8]

The nineteenth-century Dutch theologian and statesman Abraham Kuyper struck a somewhat more moderate note. Arguing for "sphere sovereignty," he saw three spheres—the Church, the State, and Society—each distinct but interrelated with the others, all part of the created order, all governed by God. "Instead of monastic flight from the world," Kuyper wrote, "the duty is now emphasized of serving God in the world, in every position of life."[9]

Like Kuyper, the twentieth-century theologian Karl Barth also took a relatively benign view of the state, believing that it, like the church, served Christ's divine purposes beyond simply restraining evil. Reinhold Niebuhr, one of the most influential twentieth-century articulators of the church-state relationship, believed in the necessity of politics in the struggle for social justice, even as he understood the sobering limitations of politics in this fallen world.

As we have seen, in historical experience, one can discern an ever-swinging pendulum of political engagement. Consider, in modern times, a single American denomination—the Baptists. For a long period, many Baptists were led by their dispensational theology to concentrate on winning souls instead of engaging the world. But it was also from within their ranks that ministers and activists like Jerry Falwell would emerge to argue for restoring America's "moral sanity" as an urgent Christian imperative. "Conservative Fundamentalists and Evangelicals can be used of God to bring about a great revival of true Christianity in America and the world in our lifetime," Falwell wrote in 1981.[10] This is a story we will return to.

STATECRAFT AS SOULCRAFT

What, then, are the views and insights we ourselves bring to this matter? How do we think Christians should approach matters of politics and governing?

To begin with, we reject the notion that Christianity and politics are at odds or irreconcilable. This is a form of Christian privatism. It has more in common with the ancient Gnostic view that creation is inherently evil than it does with the injunctions and teachings of the Hebrew Bible and the New Testament.

As all human activity—from the mundane to the profound, from personal lives to professional careers—falls under God's domain, so authentic Christian faith should be relevant to the whole of life; it ought not to be segregated from worldly affairs. "All our merely natural activities will be accepted," C. S. Lewis said, "if they are offered to God, even the humblest, and all of them, even the noblest, will be sinful if they are not. Christianity does not simply replace our natural life and substitute a new one; it is rather a new organisation which exploits, to its own supernatural end, these natural materials."[11]

We readily stipulate that, according to Christian teaching, the main purposes God wants to advance are non-political. As we saw earlier, the New Testament itself contains very little discussion of politics, and no obvious political philosophy. Christianity's core concerns have to do with soteriology (the doctrine of salvation) and eschatology (the doctrine of final things such as death and the last judgment), with the cultivation of personal virtues, and with the rules that ought to govern the behavior of individuals and the community of believers.

But God also cares about justice. And as Augustine wrote, politics can be a means through which justice—"the end of government" in the words of James Madison—is either advanced or impeded. Does this mean that the church is wrong to model itself as an alternative to this world? Not at all. But that model should not be understood as counseling subordination or powerlessness in the face of evil.

The sociologist James Davison Hunter grapples with the possibilities of political engagement in his book *To Change the World: The Irony, Tragedy, and Possibility of Christianity in the Late Modern World*. In speaking about his book, Hunter has raised a number of questions about how much we can expect politics to accomplish.

> What the state can't do is provide fully satisfying solutions to the problem of values in our society. There are no comprehensive political solutions to the deterioration of family values, the desire for equity, or the challenge of achieving consensus and solidarity in a cultural context of fragmentation and polarization. There are no real political solutions to the absence of decency, or to the spread of vulgarity.[12]

Hunter concedes that laws "do reflect values." But, he insists, laws "cannot generate values or instill values, or settle the conflict over values."[13] Therefore, he urges Christians to be "silent for a season" and "learn how to enact their faith in public through acts of shalom rather than to try again to represent it publicly through law, policy, and political mobilization."[14]

Hunter is a thoughtful and fair-minded analyst, and measured in his conclusions. But he imputes too little influence to the state and the political process. They are more important than he thinks.

"A polity is a river of constantly changing composition," George Will wrote in *Statecraft as Soulcraft*, "and the river's banks are built of laws."[15] The laws of a nation embody its values and shape them, in ways large and small, obvious and subtle, direct and indirect, sometimes immediately and often lasting. The most obvious examples from our own history concern slavery and segregation, but there are plenty of others, from welfare to education, from crime to drug use, to Supreme Court decisions like *Dred Scott v. Sandford*, *Brown v. Board of Education of Topeka*, and *Roe v. Wade*.

Laws express moral beliefs and judgments. Like throwing a pebble into a pond, the waves ripple outward. They tell citizens what our society ought to value and condemn, what is worthy of our esteem and what merits our disapprobation. They both ratify and stigmatize. That is not all that laws do, but it is among the most important things they do.

Suppose that, next year, all fifty states decide to legalize marijuana and cocaine use, prostitution and same-sex marriage. Regardless of where you stand on the issues, do you doubt that, if such laws stayed in effect for fifty years, they wouldn't fundamentally alter our views, including our moral views, of these issues? The welfare laws that passed in the 1960s helped create a culture of dependency among the underclass—and the passage of welfare reform in 1996 started to reverse it. Rudy Giuliani's policies in the 1990s helped transform New York, not only making it a far safer city, but radically improving its spirit and ethos.

Hunter is right that neither politics nor the state can "provide fully satisfying solutions to the problem of values in our society." *Nothing* can provide fully satisfying solutions to the problem of values in our society. The question is the degree to which perennial human problems can be ameliorated, and attitudes and habits thereby improved. A civilized society takes that task seriously. The work is done in our nation by many different institutions, from the family to school, from houses of worship to Hollywood, from professional sports to the military. Each has a role to play, and so does the state. Indeed, the state can have, for good or ill, a major influence on the others.

Politics and governing is fraught with temptations and dangers. There are plenty of people who bring dishonor to the enterprise. But there is also something ennobling about it when done properly. We cannot neglect the importance of our laws because we cannot neglect their influence on our moral lives. Such are the duties of citizenship in a free society.

FIVE GUIDING PRECEPTS

"Thy kingdom come, Thy will be done in earth, as it is in heaven" are the words of the Lord's Prayer. Orthodox Christianity has never held that, before His return, God's kingdom will reign here on earth. The most just political regime is incomplete and imperfect compared with what is to come. But there are degrees of incomplete and imperfect, and these carry significant consequences; to acknowledge the limitations of an earthly kingdom cannot be an excuse for passivity. Political regimes fall on a continuum, and it matters a great deal if a regime is closer to establishing a thriving democracy than to establishing a tyranny.

True, Christian engagement with politics has its own potential drawbacks, among them a discrediting of the institutional church and its basic purposes, which continue to be salvific and personal in nature. In the quest to find the right balance, there is a need for guiding precepts to help shape our thinking and actions. We offer five.

Moral Duties

First, the moral duties placed on individuals are, in important respects, different from the ones placed on the state. The Sermon on the Mount presents profound moral teachings that ought to guide the lives of individual Christians; but it was not intended to be the basis for a political philosophy or a model of how the state ought to act.

The reason is fairly obvious: the state has powers and responsibilities that are different from, and sometimes denied to, individuals. The Bible in Romans 13 makes it clear that, for Christians and non-Christians alike, government is divinely sanctioned by God to preserve public order. But if we were simplistically to apply the standards of the individual to the practices of the state, we would end up arguing that, because individuals are called to "turn the other cheek," the state should do the same—thereby making the criminal-justice system unworkable and invasions by foreign powers inevitable. Because we must not murder, should a nation never, under any circumstances, go to war?

Collapsing this distinction represents a fundamental misunderstanding of the role of government, which has invested in it powers of life, death, and coercion denied to individuals. These are powers that unfortunately are too often abused; sorting through matters of war and peace involves difficult moral choices, as we ourselves experienced during our White House years. Yet the same powers can be used to defend innocent lives and establish social order. They can also create the conditions that allow the church to exist, Christians to minister, and good works to be done. This is the reason why the callings of soldier, policeman, and president are not just permissible for Christians, but honorable.

We speak as two who have worked as representatives of the state during times of crisis and deadly attack. We were serving in the Bush White House on September 11, 2001. The day began quietly enough. One of us (Wehner) attended the 7:30 a.m. senior staff meeting in the Roosevelt Room and sent the other (Gerson) an e-mail at 8:41 a.m. Eastern time. "Very little of note happened. The economy dominated the discussions, but little new was said. Senior staff should plan to attend at least some of tonight's congressional barbecue."

At 8:46 a.m., American Airlines Flight 11 flew into the North Tower of the World Trade Center in New York City. Seventeen minutes later, at 9:03 a.m., came the second strike, when United Airlines Flight 175 crashed into the South Tower.

America was at war.

That event underscored for us, in a way nothing else really could, that we had obligations not as individuals but as public servants. We had a solemn duty to protect those whom we had taken an oath to defend, and we took it seriously. What had been an abstract debate for us was suddenly very real.

Three days later, with thousands of Americans dead and many thousands more stricken with grief, President Bush spoke at the National Cathedral. "We are here in the middle hour of our grief," he began.

> So many have suffered so great a loss, and today we express our nation's sorrow. We come before God to pray for the missing and the dead, and for those who loved them. . . . Now come the names, the list of casualties we are only beginning to read. They are the names of men and women who began their day at a desk or in an airport, busy with life. They are the names of people who faced death and in their last moments called home to say, be brave, and I love you. . . . To the children and parents and spouses and families and friends of the lost, we offer the deepest sympathy of the nation.

One of the responsibilities of the president is to speak to the nation in times of grief and sorrow. George W. Bush did that on September 14, with remarkable poise and grace. His words helped to bind together a nation that was still in shock. Yet at that moment he resolved, as did we, that we would do all we could to prevent another attack, another massacre, another event commemorating the dead. We did not want the president to once again have to offer the deepest sympathy of the nation to the children and parents and spouses and families and friends of the lost.

We were not in a mood to turn the other cheek; and we did not feel then, and we do not feel now, that this violated our consciences as Christians.

The Institutional Church and Individual Christians

Second, the institutional church has roles and responsibilities distinct from those of individual Christians.

In a recent issue of *Christianity Today*, Richard Mouw, the president of Fuller Theological Seminary, published an article titled, "Carl Henry Was Right."[16] It seems that, back in the late 1960s, Mouw, then a PhD student in philosophy, had submitted an essay describing his alienation from evangelicalism because of what he viewed as its failure to properly address issues raised by the civil rights struggle and the Vietnam War. "As a corrective," Mouw says, "I wanted the church, *as church*, to acknowledge its obligation to speak to such matters."

Carl Henry, then the magazine's editor, liked the essay but wanted one important revision: the church, he said, should regularly articulate *general* principles bearing on social concerns, while leaving it to individuals to apply those principles in particular cases. Henry's view was that the church should limit its role to negative pronouncements: it could and should say no to things socially and morally troublesome but had no mandate, jurisdiction, or competence to endorse political legislation or military tactics or economic specifics in the name of Christ.[17]

More than forty years after their exchange, Mouw writes, "There were times, I was convinced, that the church could rightly say a bold 'yes' to specific policy-like solutions. I now see that youthful conviction as misguided. Henry was right, and I was wrong."

Mouw's concession is both gracious and warranted. Individual Christians and the corporate body of Christ are not synonymous. To act otherwise is to get both into trouble. Moreover, to recognize the distinction between the responsibilities proper to the church and proper to the individual is to dignify the role of the layperson and ennoble the call of the citizen.

How so? Individual Christian laypeople may well possess special competence in a policy area—like health care or welfare, national security affairs or overseas development, legal philosophy or immigration policy—that the church simply doesn't possess and shouldn't be expected to possess. In this context, the role of the church, at least as we interpret it, is to provide individual Christians with a moral framework through which they can work out their duties as citizens and engage the world in a thoughtful way, even as it resists the temptation to instruct them on how to do their job or on which specific public policies they ought to embrace.

Scripture and Forms of Government

Third, Scripture does not provide a governing blueprint.

The New Testament gives instructions on how to pray, on how congregations should function and deacons should manage their households, on how husbands and wives should treat each other, and how to care for the aged. Yet it says almost nothing at all about what we would consider public policy.

This may be, in part, because of the circumstances in which Christians found themselves at the time the New Testament was written; Rome, after all, was largely hostile to the early followers of Jesus. But whatever the reason, Scripture simply does not offer detailed guidance on (to name just a handful of contemporary issues) trade; education; welfare; crime; health care; affirmative action; immigration; foreign aid; legal reform; drilling in the Arctic region in Alaska; climate change; and much else. And even on issues that many Christians believe the Bible does speak to, if sometimes indirectly—including poverty and wealth, abortion and same-sex marriage, capital punishment and euthanasia—nothing in the text speaks to the nature or extent of legislation or the kind of prudential steps that ought to be pursued.

Whether the top marginal tax rate should be 70 percent, 40 percent, or 28 percent is a serious public policy issue—but neither the New Testament nor the Hebrew Bible sheds light on the matter. One may believe we have a scriptural obligation to be good stewards of the earth—but that doesn't necessarily determine where one will stand on the Kyoto Protocol or cap-and-trade legislation. A person can take to heart the admonition in Exodus not to "oppress a stranger"—and still grapple with the issue of whether to grant a path to citizenship to illegal immigrants. Nor does the Bible tell us whether the 1991 Gulf War was the right or wrong decision.

The Christian ethicist Paul Ramsey has written,

> Identification of Christian social ethics with specific partisan proposals that clearly are not the only ones that may be characterized as Christian and as morally acceptable comes close to the original New Testament meaning of *heresy.*[18]

Such identification can also be discrediting. Many mainline denominations, like the Presbyterian Church (USA) and the Episcopal Church, have badly damaged their credibility by taking stands on a staggering number of issues to which they have brought no special competence or insight but have simply parroted standard liberal/left talking points. The same can be said, on the other side, of the Christian Coalition, which handed out political "scorecards" and voters' guides to congregants before elections. "What has happened, time and time again," warns the Catholic scholar George Weigel, "is that an increasingly partisan public profile ends up stripping an organization of religiously based moral content."[19]

On the other hand—and it is an important other hand—Christians as well as people of other faiths *are* provided with moral precepts that ought to guide them in pursuing justice and peace, human dignity and the moral good. If their careers happen to be in government, how should they go about it?

This is very tricky territory. People involved in public service need to determine as best they can what is the correct stand on an array of issues and what issues deserve to be given priority. We all recognize a hierarchy of moral concern, according to which matters like war, slavery, poverty, and the protection of innocent life occupy a higher plane than questions of mass transit and funding for public television. And most of us can agree that under certain circumstances, not only individual Christians but the church itself should speak out in specific ways against specific evils. But in the vast majority of cases, what we are talking about are prudential judgments about competing priorities, and we need to approach them with humility and open minds.

Honorable people have honest disagreements. Some reflect hard on what is right and find themselves coming down on the "liberal" side of things. Others reflect hard and find themselves coming down on the "conservative" side. Yet to govern is to choose—and those in public life have a duty to develop, as best they can, a sound political philosophy, to engage in rigorous moral reasoning, and to make sure they do not become so captive to ideology that they ignore empirical evidence. And then they have to pursue policies that they believe are right and wise.

Political Involvement Takes Various Forms

Fourth, the form of political involvement adopted by Christian citizens is determined in part by the nature of the society in which they live.

If one lives in a thriving democracy, the duties of citizenship take a particular form. They range from paying taxes to voting, from serving in government to petitioning it, from speaking out in public forums to attending rallies and protests. Government is the "offspring of our own choice," President Washington said in his Farewell Address—one that "has a just claim to [our] confidence and [our] support."

People participating in a democratic process also need to abide by certain rules. Among them is accepting that on particular issues—including those on which one may have deep moral convictions—an individual may lose; and when defeat occurs, the verdict needs to be accepted. This does not mean one must agree with the decision, let alone consider it final; there are no closed questions in an open society. Even when the highest court in the land issues a judgment, the matter is not necessarily settled. We saw that with the *Dred Scott* decision and with *Roe v. Wade.* Citizens in a self-governing nation need to abide by the laws even as they seek to change them. In a republic like ours, this is a duty of citizenship.

But suppose one lived in an absolute monarchy, a police state, or an Iranian-style theocracy. Obviously one could have far less influence on the actions of the regime itself, and the duties of citizenship would be quite different. An individual might become a dissident—in some cases, a martyr. But at what point *should* a Christian rise up against a state that is illegal and illegitimate, and that engages in acts that are intrinsically evil? That is not so clear, and once again we are faced with scriptural verses that are difficult to reconcile.

In the book of 1 Peter, Christians are told to obey even unjust masters, for doing so provides a powerful witness. In his letter to the Christians in Rome, St. Paul wrote, "Everyone must submit himself to the governing authorities." (The governing authority then was Nero, who persecuted Christians and burned them at the stake.) Yet Christians are also taught that, if they are ever in conflict, their duty to God is higher than their duty to the state. "We must obey God rather than men," St. Peter asserts when the apostles are forbidden to evangelize. Much depends on the exact nature of the historical circumstances, and on individuals' sense of duty and responsibility.

Dietrich Bonhoeffer was a German Lutheran pastor and theologian during the time of Adolf Hitler's rise to power. His American friends helped him escape in 1939, but he felt he had to return to

Germany in order to be in solidarity with persecuted Christians there. "I shall have no right . . . to participate in the reconstruction of Christian life in Germany after the war if I do not share the trials of this time with my people," Bonhoeffer wrote to his friend Reinhold Niebuhr.[20] An avowed pacifist, Bonhoeffer joined an organization that was at the heart of the anti-Hitler resistance, became an advocate for the assassination of the Nazi dictator, and was eventually executed for his role in the plot. The camp doctor who witnessed the execution wrote,

> I saw Pastor Bonhoeffer . . . kneeling on the floor praying fervently to his God. I was most deeply moved by the way this unusually lovable man prayed, so devout and so certain that God heard his prayer. At the place of execution, he again said a short prayer and then climbed the steps to the gallows, brave and composed. His death ensued after a few seconds. In the almost fifty years that I worked as a doctor, I have hardly ever seen a man die so entirely submissive to the will of God.[21]

Bonhoeffer's decision reflects "the finest logic of Christian martyrdom," Niebuhr declared, and belongs "to the modern Acts of the Apostles."[22]

Of us, living in the United States, martyrdom is not demanded. Being informed and engaged, acting decently and respectfully toward others, is quite enough.

Ancient Israel Is Not the Paradigm

Fifth, God does not deal with nations today as He did with ancient Israel.

Orthodox Christians believe, as do many Jews, that the Jews are a chosen people—chosen to be in a covenant with God and called as witnesses of a true faith among the nations. "For you are a people holy to the Lord your God. The Lord your God has chosen you out of all the peoples on the face of the earth to be his people, his treasured possession," the book of Deuteronomy says.

The story of the Jews begins with Abraham, who left Mesopotamia for a land God called him to. In calling Abraham, God made a divine covenant that promised him a land, divine protection, and progeny as numerous as the sands of the shore. A later covenant at Sinai with the people of Israel specified rewards and punishments based on their faithfulness and conduct.

This needs to be set against other teachings and books in the Bible, including Job, where it seems that the sufferings that would befall Israel were not *solely* dependent on, or a consequence of, their moral behavior. Still, there was a belief in *communal* righteousness—that the sins of the few could lead to the punishment of the many. This in turn created a common ethic among the Hebrew people, an investment by all of its members in the integrity of the community.

Throughout American history, some people, especially the Puritans, believed that something similar applied to America. They believed that America, like Israel before it, had received a special calling from God, that it was set apart for divine purposes. Americans, too, were a "chosen people," and America was seen as the "new" Israel, "entrusted with the responsibility of establishing a 'righteous empire' or a Christian commonwealth."[23] For some, the logical corollary was that God would therefore deal with America just as He had dealt with Israel, dispensing blessings and curses according to its moral conduct.

We have seen this view articulated many times over the years—including in the comments of Pat Robertson in the aftermath of a catastrophic earthquake in Haiti. In the judgment of the Reverend Robertson, Haitians had been "cursed by one thing after another" since they "swore a pact to the devil" in order to free themselves from their subjugation to the French.

However, this view simply melts under scrutiny. For one thing, it is exceedingly arrogant for an individual to believe he can discern the will of God and determine whether a particular tragedy is a manifestation of His judgment. For another, it raises a host of practical problems. Why would God's wrath be directed toward America or Haiti, but not, say, Iran (a repressive Islamic theocracy), North Korea (a brutal police state), or China (a Communist nation that coerces women to have abortions)? What exactly are the sins that serve as the tripwire to divine wrath? Abortion and gay marriage—or wars and indifference to poverty? Removing God from the classroom—or not welcoming illegal aliens into our country? Is God's judgment a response to outward behavior (e.g., infidelity) or to the inward spirit (e.g., pride and arrogance)?

One can see how this line of thinking—whether in the simplistic, connect-the-dots version offered up by the Reverend Robertson or in the more moderate views held by millions of other Christians—can lead one into a thicket of confusion.

On a deeper level, we believe this interpretation of national sowing-and-reaping doesn't correspond with a proper understanding of Christianity. While the Bible teaches God has judged nations, nowhere does it assume that all suffering is a sign of God's displeasure. In fact, the most important symbol in Christianity is the cross, which represents suffering, agony, and death. Speaking to Ananias, who was instrumental in the conversion of St. Paul, Jesus says, "I will show [Paul] how much he must suffer for my name." St. Paul himself, in the book of Timothy, writes, "Everyone who wants to live a godly life in Christ Jesus will be persecuted." St. Peter speaks about the suffering that Christians will endure for doing good. And in the book of Romans we read that we are to rejoice in our suffering because it produces perseverance, and perseverance produces character, and character produces hope.

We ourselves don't pretend to understand how and why God acts in tragic events and are skeptical of those who claim they do. Such interpretations are certainly not self-evident.

Christians must reconcile their conviction that Jesus cares

deeply for us and is involved in the affairs of man with suffering and tragedy writ small and writ large. It isn't an easy thing to come to grips with. Even C. S. Lewis, a monumental figure in twentieth-century Christianity, saw his faith buckle for a time after the death of his wife, Joy (Lewis eventually recovered, though he was clearly a different man). "Not that I am (I think) in much danger of ceasing to believe in God," Lewis wrote in piercing words. "The real danger is of coming to believe such dreadful things about Him. The conclusion I dread is not 'So there's no God after all,' but 'So this is what God's really like. Deceive yourself no longer.'"[24]

What the Christian faith teaches us is that even in suffering there can be redemption; that this world, for all of its joys and sorrows, is not our home; and that at the end of our pilgrimage, beyond the sufferings of this world, there are streams of mercy, never ceasing.

SORTING THROUGH THE CHOICES

The world is a "theater of [God's] glory," John Calvin said,[25] and we are all actors in His unfolding drama and His redemptive purposes. Politics can therefore be a noble and important undertaking. Yet determining the precise nature of our involvement is no easy task. It depends on facts and circumstances, and it requires judgment and wisdom, discretion and humility. Some who have gone before us have gotten the balance just right, and many others have gotten it terribly wrong. It is a road some are called upon to travel, but it is filled with traps and snares. The good that Christians in politics can do is considerable, and the collateral damage politics can do to the Christian faith is substantial.

There is no easy shortcut, no prepackaged formula, that tells Christians when to get involved in politics and when to pull back, when speaking out on public matters will help or hurt their Christian witness. This side of the heavenly city, we can only peer through a glass darkly. One day the clouds will part and all things will become clear. Until then, our obligation is to sort through, even in an imperfect way, the choices before us; to seek the counsel of people of wisdom and integrity; to examine and re-examine our motives and the state of our hearts; continually to revisit our approach and stance in light of events; and to pray, in the words of the author of Colossians, that God will fill us with the knowledge of His will through all spiritual wisdom and understanding.

NOTES

1. Jacques Ellul, *False Presence of the Kingdom* (New York: Seabury Press, 1972), 126.

2. J. Philip Wogaman, *Christian Perspectives on Politics* (Philadelphia: Fortress Press, 1988), 127.

3. Robert E. Webber, *The Church in the World* (Grand Rapids: Academie Books, 1986), 64.

4. St. Augustine, *City of God*, ed. Gerald G. Walsh, Demetrius B. Zema, Grace Monahan, and Daniel J. Honan (Garden City: Image Books, 1958), 88.

5. Webber, *The Church in the World*, 71.

6. Martin Luther, "Temporal Authority," in *Luther's Works*, quoted in Webber, *The Church in the World*, 108.

7. Webber, *The Church in the World*, 127.

8. Ibid., 132–33.

9. Irving Hexham, "Christian Politics according to Abraham Kuyper," *CRUX* 19, no. 1, March 1983: 2–7, http://people.ucalgary.ca/~nurelweb/papers/irving/kuyperp.html.

10. Jerry Falwell, "The Fundamentalist Phenomenon," with Ed Dobson and Ed Hindson, in *Piety & Politics: Evangelicals and Fundamentalists Confront the World*, ed. Richard John Neuhaus and Michael Cromartie, (Washington, D.C.: Ethics and Public Policy Center, 1987), 123.

11. C. S. Lewis, "Learning in Wartime," in *The Weight of Glory* (Grand Rapids: Eerdmans, 1949), 48.

12. The Faith Angle Conference on Religion, Politics & Public Life, "Event Transcript: To Change the World: The Irony, Tragedy, and Possibility of Christianity in the Late Modern World," Ethics and Public Policy Center, http://www.eppc.org/publications/pubID.4125/pub_detail.asp.

13. Ibid.

14. James Davison Hunter, *To Change the World: The Irony, Tragedy & Possibility of Christianity in the Late Modern World* (New York: Oxford University Press, 2010), 281.

15. George F. Will, *Statecraft as Soulcraft: What Government Does* (New York: Simon & Schuster, 1983), 66.

16. Richard J. Mouw, "Carl Henry Was Right," *Christianity Today* 54, no. 1 (January 27, 2010), http://www.christianitytoday.com/ct/2010/january/25.30.html.

17. Carl F. H. Henry, *Confessions of a Theologian* (Waco: World Books, 1986), 270–71.

18. Mouw, "Carl Henry Was Right."

19. George Weigel et al., *Disciples & Democracy*, ed. Michael Cromartie (Washington, D.C.: Ethics and Public Policy Center, 1994), 34–35.

20. Dietrich Bonhoeffer, *The Cost of Discipleship* (New York: Macmillan, 1949), 16.

21. Eberhard Bethge, *Dietrich Bonhoeffer: A Biography* (Minneapolis: Fortress Press, 2000), 927.

22. Bonhoeffer, *The Cost of Discipleship*, 16, 33.

23. James Davison Hunter, "American Evangelicalism: Conservative Religion and the Quandary of Modernity" (1983), in *Piety & Politics: Evangelicals and Fundamentalists Confront the World*, ed. Richard John Neuhaus and Michael Cromartie, (Washington, D.C.: Ethics and Public Policy Center, 1987), 23.

24. C. S. Lewis, *A Grief Observed* (New York: Seabury Press, 1961), 5.

25. Webber, *The Church in the World*, 127.

CHAPTER TWO

The Religious Right

For quite a long time, as we noted briefly in the previous chapter, Christian fundamentalists and evangelicals in this country kept their distance from active engagement with politics. This quiescent attitude was in keeping with the deeply held conviction that their proper business was saving souls, not saving the world. But, inadvertently, their aloofness also served the political purposes of secularists bent on using the courts to advance their own social and cultural agenda—an agenda inimical to the moral values, and the family interests, of millions of Americans. The result: a Christian movement, at first reluctant and then increasingly robust, to mobilize a religiously conservative counterweight to the regnant ideology of secular liberalism.

It would be hard to pinpoint the moment when this movement was born, but Michael Cromartie of the Ethics and Public Policy Center has pointed to when it discovered its own influence. The time was 1976, and Jimmy Carter, a Southern evangelical, was the newly nominated presidential candidate of the Democratic party. In a lengthy interview with *Playboy* magazine, Carter admitted, "I've looked on a lot of women with lust."[1] This provoked a public criticism of the candidate by the independent Baptist minister Jerry Falwell—not for having admitted to "lust," a commonplace evangelical confession—but for having granted an interview to, of all places, *Playboy*. Much to Falwell's surprise, his criticism elicited a phone call from Carter's aide, Jody Powell, demanding that the pastor refrain from criticizing the Democratic candidate.

For Falwell, this was a vivid sign that American politics at the highest level would respond to the concerns of activist religious leaders voicing moral misgivings. This was the same Falwell who in 1965 had declared, "I would find it impossible to stop preaching the pure saving Gospel of Jesus Christ and begin doing anything else—including fighting communism, or participating in civil-rights reforms."[2] At another point he had said, "We have few ties to this earth. We pay our taxes, cast our votes as a responsibility of citizenship, obey the laws of the land, and other things demanded of us by the society in which we live. But, at the same time, we are cognizant that our only purpose on the earth is to know Christ and to make him known."[3] Now, Falwell was organizing "I Love America" rallies on the steps of state capitols. By 1979, he would found the Moral Majority. During the 1980 presidential election, he pledged to mobilize voters for Ronald Reagan, "even if he has the devil running with him."

Among many religious conservatives, the transformation from separatists to activists had been swift and complete.

Liberal reaction came no less swiftly. In 1984, Democratic presidential candidate Walter Mondale made fear of the religious right a centerpiece of his campaign against the incumbent Ronald Reagan. In a television ad sponsored by the Mondale campaign, a picture of Reagan and Falwell appeared on an engraved invitation. A voice intoned,

> Ronald Reagan and Rev. Jerry Falwell cordially invite you to their
> party on Nov. 6. Here's all you have to believe in: the secret war in
> Central America. All new Supreme Court Justices must rule abor-
> tion is a crime even in the case of rape and incest. No Equal Rights
> Amendment. No mutually verifiable nuclear freeze.[4]

The ad concluded, "Think about the people who have taken
over the Republican party. They want their new platform to be your
new Constitution. Think about that."

Very early on, the pattern of such hyperbole and fear-monger-
ing was set. Democratic officials expressed surprise and fright at
the very existence of religious conservatives in America. Here was
Patricia Harris, Secretary of Health and Human Services under
President Carter: "I am beginning to fear that we could have an
Ayatollah Khomeini in this country, but he will not have a beard,
... He will have a television program."[5] And here was the liberal
journalist Sidney Blumenthal: "In preparing for the universal apocalypse, the movement evangelicals are eagerly pursuing an ideological apocalypse. The business of soul winning has become the
politics of takeover."[6]

Democratic campaign consultants were quick to seize upon
leaders of the religious right as foils—or as one Mondale aide referred to Falwell, "no-risk whipping boy[s]."[7] Unintentionally, and
in the way of politics, the heightened criticism raised these religious leaders' profiles and increased their fund-raising capabilities.
Meanwhile, the media—thoroughly enjoying the resulting skir-
mishes—amplified the most strident voices. America's contemporary "culture wars" had begun in earnest.

FROM ACTIVISM TO DISENGAGEMENT TO ACTIVISM

Largely lost in these debates was an appreciation of the history and
diversity of conservative religion in America.

About seventy years prior to the founding of the Moral Majority, the Democratic nominee for the presidency had been the nation's most prominent evangelical. William Jennings Bryan was both the leader of the populist, progressive wing of his party—a supporter of the graduated income tax, women's suffrage, and the regulation of child labor—and an outspoken, conservative Christian. But Bryan eventually came to symbolize the shattering of the evangelical-progressive alliance.

During the Scopes trial in 1925, in which he argued against the teaching of evolution in schools, Bryan, by then a former presidential nominee and Secretary of State, became an object of scorn and derision among cultural and media elites. The journalist H. L. Mencken characterized fundamentalism as a "childish theology" for "halfwits." Conservative Christians were the "anthropoid rabble" and the "gaping primates of the upland valleys." "Christendom," wrote Mencken in the mid-1920s, "may be defined briefly as that part of the world in which, if any man stands up in public and solemnly swears that he is a Christian, all his auditors will laugh."[8]

In this same period, mainline Protestant denominations became invested in a "social gospel" defined as the pursuit of justice in this world. In reaction, many theological conservatives went entirely in the other direction, emphasizing the world's irredeemable corruption, and many churches and denominations stressed personal piety at the expense of social engagement. For conservative Christians, this was a time of cultural isolation and irrelevance. "Within the span of one generation," the historian George Marsden has written, "this extraordinary influence of evangelicalism in the public sphere of American culture collapsed."[9]

It took a few decades for important evangelical figures to begin calling for cultural reengagement. In 1947, in *The Uneasy Conscience of Modern Fundamentalism*, the theologian Carl Henry (whom we have already met in chapter 1) urged Christians to confront societal ills in political partnership with nonbelievers. "While it is not the Christian's task to correct social, moral and political conditions as his primary effort," wrote Henry, "he ought to lend his endorsement to remedial efforts in *any context not specifically anti-redemptive*"[10] (emphasis added). Henry was calling, in short, for at least a partial reversal of the great evangelical retreat.

The figure who gave conservative Christians a more winsome face in the broader culture was the evangelist Billy Graham. His message was not primarily political, but he became a confessor of sorts to Presidents Dwight Eisenhower, Lyndon Johnson, and Richard Nixon. Although Graham was burned by these close associations, especially with Nixon, throughout the 1950s, '60s, and early '70s, he created a distinctive model for evangelical social engagement: bipartisan, inclusive of Catholics, and slightly naïve. Indeed, Graham's moderation aroused controversy among some segments of the conservative Christian population. Grant Wacker describes the split vividly: "An evangelical is someone who really, really likes Billy Graham and a fundamentalist is someone who thinks Billy Graham is a liberal."[11]

This points to a frequently overlooked characteristic of activist, conservative religion in America: it has always taken more than a single form. In 1973, in one early sign of social re-engagement, forty prominent evangelical leaders, including Carl Henry, met to sign the "Chicago Declaration of Evangelical Social Concern." It read, in part: "Although the Lord calls us to defend the social and economic rights of the poor and oppressed, we have mostly remained silent. We deplore the historic involvement of the church in America with racism and the conspicuous responsibility of the evangelical community for perpetuating the personal attitudes and institutional structures that have divided the body of Christ along color lines."[12] In 1977, Ron Sider, another signer of the Chicago Declaration, published his enormously influential *Rich Christians in an Age of Hunger*, analyzing the causes of poverty and calling Christians to live more simply.

If that was one face of re-engagement, another and, as it turned out, much more influential one was the one we referred to in the opening paragraphs of this chapter. Beginning in the late 1960s, Christian conservatives experienced a massive cultural shock: a rapid, disorienting change in American morals and customs. A series of societal shifts, government actions, and court decisions, all mutually reinforcing, struck many Christian conservatives as a coordinated assault on their communities and their values. The banning of school prayer and Bible reading, the declaration of a constitutional right to abortion on demand, attacks on the freedom of religious day schools, the prevalence of pornography and recreational drug use, and the growth of out-of-wedlock births offended and appalled Christian believers.

Contrary to later charges that conservative Christians like Falwell were seeking to "impose their views" on other Americans, they actually saw themselves as victims of an elite culture determined to impose its views on *them*. "It is the great successes of secular and liberal forces," argued the sociologist Nathan Glazer at the time, "principally operating through the specific agency of the courts, that has in large measure created the issues on which the fundamentalists have managed to achieve what influence they have."[13] This defensive reaction, in turn, caused exaggerated liberal counterattacks of the kind we documented earlier.

For the conservative, cultural resistance was not supposed to happen. Had not fundamentalism been buried as a cultural force way back in the 1920s? Academic theories of secularization asserted that conservative religion would fade away, as it seemed to have done in Europe. Science left little need for the explanations of faith. Modernity *meant* secularism. But, in America, it did not work out that way.

Thus it was that skilled religious entrepreneurs like Falwell were able to organize and channel the conservative reaction against the 1960s into a movement. A generation of religious activists created what the scholar George Marsden calls a "transdenominational community": a network of colleges, ministries, and other institutions making effective use of television, radio, and direct mail and applying sophisticated technologies to the promotion of traditional values.

VARIETIES OF ENGAGEMENT

How, though, has the influence of the religious conservatives been exercised, and to what effect?

Within the modern evangelical movement there have been at least three different styles of engagement. In shorthand, they may be described as the priest, the prophet, and the kingmaker.

Billy Graham has acted as the priest and confessor of American democracy—a fixture at public ceremonies like presidential inaugurals and services of national mourning. For decades he has maintained a clear Christian witness.

In contrast, James Dobson, the founder of Focus on the Family, has assumed the role of prophet. On issues relating to the upbringing of children, Dobson's tone tends to be quiet and measured; in politics, however, he has a long-standing habit of issuing thundering demands and denunciations, only to threaten to pick up his political marbles and go home. "If neither of the two major political parties nominates an individual who pledges himself or herself to the sanctity of human life," Dobson has said, "we will join others in voting for a minor-party candidate."[14] Or again, "Does the Republican Party want our votes, no strings attached—to court us every two years, and then say, 'Don't call me; I'll call you'—and not care about the moral law of the universe? . . . Is this the way it's going to be? If it is, I'm gone, and if I go, I will do everything I can to take as many people with me as possible."[15]

Then there is Pat Robertson, the founder of the Christian Broadcasting Network and the Christian Coalition. The son of a conservative Democratic senator, Robertson has sought to be a Republican kingmaker, even running for president himself in 1988 and later setting out to be a grassroots political force. Of the

Christian Coalition, he has said, "We are training people to be effective—to be elected to school boards, to city councils, to state legislatures and to key positions in political parties. . . . If we work and give and organize and train, the Christian Coalition will be the most powerful political organization in America."[16] Robertson's main emphasis has often fallen on strategy, i.e., "electability," rather than on ideological purity. Thus, during the 2008 presidential primaries he endorsed former New York City mayor Rudolph Giuliani, a candidate who supported both abortion and gay rights.

Each of these styles exhibits drawbacks as well as strengths. Graham's effectiveness has occasionally been compromised by uncritical associations with the powerful. Dobson's approach—afflicting and intimidating the powerful—is of demonstrably questionable utility. Robertson's role as Republican kingmaker has been undercut by his habit of making embarrassing and offensive statements of one kind or another. Of the three, however, Robertson undeniably contributed a grassroots political sophistication to the religious right—along with the recognition that compromise is sometimes necessary to build winning political coalitions.

As for those coalitions, they have generally been with the GOP. This should come as no surprise. Of the two major parties, at least since the 1970s, the GOP at the national level has been the more culturally conservative. Even secular Republicans tend to stand for social order and cohesion against the expressive individualism of modern liberalism. This broad trend has been accelerated by the public disdain shown by many Democrats toward the religious right and by the Democratic Party's unqualified embrace of abortion on demand. In 1976, about 50 percent of white evangelicals voted for the GOP presidential candidate. By 1984, the figure was 76 percent—a swift and massive shift.

Party allegiances tell only one part of the story, however. As a phenomenon, the religious right has displayed a number of qualities prominently associated with a (small-d) democratic temperament. The long-time cultural separatism of many evangelicals may have been an understandable response to a hostile culture, but it also amounted to an abdication of citizenship. Starting in the 1960s, religious-right leaders led an alienated group of voters back into the public square, and they did so by employing all the traditional methods of democratic engagement: mobilizing voter-registration drives, training activists, knocking on doors, conducting marches and demonstrations. In large percentages, members of Christian-right organizations are in contact with public officials, circulate petitions, and write letters to the editor. Indeed, notes the sociologist Robert Putnam, "It is among evangelical conservatives, rather than [among] the ideological heirs of the 1960s, that we find the strongest evidence for an upwelling of civic engagement."[17]

Historically, and contrary to its detractors, another democratic quality of the religious right has been its religious inclusiveness. Falwell's Moral Majority was specifically designed to embrace Protestants, Catholics, Jews, and Mormons. The pro-life movement involved close cooperation between fundamentalists and Catholics. Establishing a political coalition based on shared moral values has required the toning down of theological exclusivity and the overcoming of old prejudices—and this has been seen most strikingly in the cooperation between evangelical Protestants and Catholics.

The historian Arthur M. Schlesinger once called prejudice against Catholics "the deepest bias in the history of the American people."[18] Following a wave of Catholic immigration in the early nineteenth century, the Know-Nothing Party preached a vicious brand of anti-Catholicism with broad social resonance. As late as 1960, though the intensity had faded, anti-Catholicism was still a serious enough issue among Protestants to cast a big question mark over John F. Kennedy's fitness as a candidate for president. Many, including the famous preacher and author Norman Vincent Peale, warned that a President Kennedy would take orders from the pope in Rome.

In light of this history, the close cooperation of evangelicals and Catholics fostered by the religious right was unprecedented. Catholic leaders like Rep. Henry Hyde and Justice Antonin Scalia became heroes to many conservative Protestants. Evangelicals respected Pope John Paul II for his pro-life convictions, opposition to Communism, and personal holiness. In 1994, the conservative Protestant leader Charles Colson and Father Richard John Neuhaus cosigned a document, "Evangelicals and Catholics Together," testifying to a broad ecumenical rapprochement. Common moral values and political concerns had at least partially overcome old theological conflicts, and the healing force, remarkably, was democratic engagement.

SUCCESSES AND FAILURES

What, finally, has the religious right achieved?

Despite many setbacks, it succeeded in mustering a broad resistance to the legal establishment of secularism. Some on the left still contend that religiously motivated arguments are illegitimate in the debate over public policy. Evidently, in their conception, the separation of church and state means that, although citizens may advocate a certain political view on the basis of utilitarianism or liberalism or vegetarianism, they may not do so on the basis of moral views rooted in Christianity or Judaism. Religious conservatives have stoutly resisted this notion, reminding us that many pivotal events in American political history—from abolition to the civil rights movement—came about in large part thanks to religiously informed social activism. They have stood for the principle that a genuine pluralism must include religious people. Even among their adversaries, this principle has attained a status long denied it in American politics and jurisprudence.

Practically speaking, the religious right has also scored some successes. When *Roe v. Wade* was decided in 1973, essentially legalizing abortion on demand, an editorial in the *New York Times* announced that the abortion debate was over. In part because of the religious right, that debate continues—with a majority of Americans in some polls now considering themselves pro-life. Given the cultural forces arrayed against pro-life Americans—from the legal system, to elite culture, to a broad social ethic of autonomy and convenience—this is a remarkable achievement.

The religious right has also formed an element in a larger political coalition defending and encouraging an active, moral role for America in the world. This was especially important during the period of the Cold War. And it has been a stalwart supporter of the often friendless state of Israel in that nation's struggle for survival against enemies sworn to its destruction. We will return to these themes in chapter 4.

How does this record stack up against the hopes held out by some conservative activists? After three decades of political engagement, they might point out, there are still only a few legal restrictions on abortion. Pornography is pervasive. Entertainment is coarser and more explicit than ever. Family structures are fragile, especially among the poor. The country seems on the verge of accepting gay marriage.

All true—but, in our opinion, such a negative judgment is too sweeping, lacking in realism as well as charity. By providing a structured opposition to cultural liberalism, religious conservatives have slowed the movement toward a permissive society and prevented the complete victory of liberal secularism. They have retarded social trends they could not wholly reverse, in the process sparking a national debate on the role of character and values in an orderly, just society. They have not transformed America into the City of God—this is not given to mortal beings to accomplish—but they have demonstrated that America is not Sweden.

LESSONS LEARNED

Still, could the religious right have done things better, and is a different model of social engagement needed for the future? We believe the answer to both questions is yes.

The language and tone of the religious right have often been apocalyptic, off-putting, and counterproductive. "Just like what Nazi Germany did to the Jews," said Falwell, "so liberal America is now doing to evangelical Christians." "Never again," intoned a mailing from the Christian Coalition, "will we be subject to a government that dishonors our Lord."[19] In 1994, a conspiracy-mongering video promoted by Falwell associated President Bill Clinton with drug dealing and murder.

Such melodrama, or hysteria, is good for fund-raising, but bad for American politics. It makes a civil political conversation impossible, and does a disservice to the cause of a Christian witness to society.

Strategically, too, the religious right has been inconsistent and politically arbitrary. During the 1980s, the Christian Voice issued report cards measuring candidates' views not only on school prayer and abortion but also on support for an American defense treaty with Taiwan and opposition to a national Department of Education; there were no categories concerning the relief of poverty or racial equality. Such selectivity left a strong impression that the movement was less an independent voice than a tool of a specific political ideology. Like the social-gospel movement of an earlier era, the religious right seemed to be baptizing someone else's political agenda instead of providing a perspective based on a different set of moral priorities. As Carl Henry put it, the religious right in the 1980s and '90s "largely forfeited the opportunity to formulate a persuasive public philosophy and to exhibit what it means to engage in politics Christianly."[20]

The biggest problem of the religious right, however, has not been tonal or strategic but theological. As we noted in the previous chapter, some conservative Christians have identified the nature and destiny of America with the nature and destiny of biblical Israel. Since the Founding Fathers "developed a nation predicated on Holy Writ," said Falwell, it has been incumbent on anyone hoping for divine favor to join in the battle to "reclaim America for Christ."[21] This view of the New World as the new Israel has a long history, but a pedigree does not make it correct.

America was not founded as a Christian nation—precisely *because* the founders were informed by a Jewish and Christian understanding of human nature. Since humans are autonomous moral beings created in God's image, freedom of conscience is essential to their dignity. At least where the federal government was concerned, the founders asserted that citizens should be subject to God and their conscience, not to the state. America was designed to be a nation where all faiths are welcomed, not one where one faith is favored. Historically, this disestablishment of religion has served the Christian faith well, preserving it from being corrupted and tainted by political power.

We dwelled earlier on the error of confusing America with ancient Israel, with the corollary that national morality alone determines divine favor. Here it will suffice to add an example of the theological and moral absurdities to which such a view can lead. Following the September 11, 2001, attacks in New York and Pennsylvania, Pat Robertson and Jerry Falwell held a televised conversation:

Falwell: *I agree totally with you that the Lord has protected us so wonderfully these 225 years. And since 1812, this is the first time that we've been attacked on our soil, first time, and by far the worst results. And I fear, as Donald Rumsfeld, the Secretary of Defense said yesterday, that this is only the beginning. And with biological warfare available to these monsters . . . what we saw on Tuesday, as terrible as it is, could be minuscule if, in*

	fact, God continues to lift the curtain and allow the enemies of America to give us probably what we deserve.
Robertson:	*Jerry, that's my feeling. I think we've just seen the antechamber to terror. We haven't even begun to see what they can do to the major population.*
Falwell:	*The ACLU's got to take a lot of blame for this.*
Robertson:	*Well, yes.*
Falwell:	*And, I know that I'll hear from them for this. But, throwing God out successfully with the help of the federal court system, throwing God out of [the] public square, out of the schools. The abortionists have got to bear some burden for this because God will not be mocked. And when we destroy 40 million little innocent babies, we make God mad. I really believe that the pagans, and the abortionists, and the feminists, and the gays and the lesbians who are actively trying to make that an alternative lifestyle, the ACLU, People for the American Way, all of them who have tried to secularize America, I point the finger in their face and say, "You helped this happen."*
Robertson:	*Well, I totally concur, and the problem is we have adopted that agenda at the highest levels of our government.*[22]

This approach is not only wrong, it puts Robertson and Falwell in company they would presumably find distasteful. Not long ago, for example, a senior Iranian cleric blamed earthquakes in his country on declining sexual standards. "Many women who do not dress modestly lead young men astray, corrupt their chastity and spread adultery in society, which increases earthquakes."[23]

In Christian belief, God's ultimate goal is to bring men and women into communion with Himself. His dealings with the world serve that purpose. And God's purpose is often advanced through redemptive suffering, which is not a punishment, but a mystery and a method of grace.

The workings of God in the midst of tragedy cannot be reduced to a simplistic moral mathematics in which sin yields disaster, precisely because America is not a covenant community on the model of ancient Israel. The community of faith is found in every nation. Believers share the blessings and tragedies of their neighbors. Rather than declaring the suffering of their neighbors to be deserved, they should work and pray for the common good.

In combination, the various failings of the religious right—of tone, strategy, theology, and simple human sympathy—abetted a social backlash that goes beyond politics. By the 1990s, argues Robert Putnam, the politicization of religion by the religious right was causing many young people to turn against religion itself. Their attitude seemed to be, "If this is religion, I'm not interested." Today, Americans in their twenties are much more secular than were the Baby Boomers at the same stage of life. In what Putnam calls a "stunning development,"[24] about 30 to 35 percent are religiously unaffiliated. The religious right, it turns out, was not good for religion.

The religious right began as a defensive reaction to the aggressions of the modern world. It ended by squandering much of its promise because it was too reactive. Often it responded to anger with anger. It responded to the liberal gospel by downplaying the very idea of social justice, thus narrowing the range of evangelical concern. The result was often a partial agenda, even a partisan one. In an unexpected way, this reactive model of social engagement allowed the left to continue setting the social and political agenda.

This is particularly the case on the issues of abortion and secularization. We believe that these two issues are vital to the character and future of the country. But they do not exhaust the Christian contribution to the City of Man. The next phase of Christian social engagement will need to move beyond reaction, instead applying first principles to a broad range of public concerns.

NOTES

1. "The Nation: Trying to Be One of the Boys," *Time*, October 4, 1976, http://www.time.com/time/magazine/article/0,9171,918397,00.html.

2. Richard J. Neuhaus, *The Naked Public Square: Religion and Democracy in America* (Grand Rapids: Eerdmans, 1986), 10.

3. A. James Reichley, "Religion and the Future of American Politics," *Political Science Quarterly*, vol. 101, no. 1 (1986), 24.

4. "Mondale's Whipping Boy," *Time*, October 22, 1984, http://www.time.com/time/magazine/article/0,9171,951323,00.html.

5. Joseph Loconte and Michael Cromartie, "Let's Stop Stereotyping Evangelicals," *Washington Post*, November 8, 2006, http://www.washingtonpost.com/wp-dyn/content/article/2006/11/07/AR2006110701228.html.

6. Sidney Blumenthal, *Our Long National Daydream: A Political Pageant of the Reagan Era* (New York: HarperCollins, 1990), 151.

7. "Mondale's Whipping Boy," *Time*, October 22, 1984, http://www.time.com/time/magazine/article/0,9171,951323,00.html.

8. H. L. Mencken, *Prejudices*, fourth series (New York: Alfred A. Knopf, 1924), 78–79, as quoted by George M. Marsden, *Reforming Fundamentalism* (Grand Rapids: Eerdmans, 1995), 123.

9. George M. Mardsen, *Reforming Fundamentalism* (Grand Rapids: Eerdmans, 1995), 4.

10. Carl Henry, *The Uneasy Conscience of Modern Fundamentalism* (Grand Rapids: Eerdmans, 1947), 87.

11. Grant Wacker, "A Conversation with Nathan Hatch, Grant Wacker, and Hanna Rosin," in *Religion and Politics in America: A Conversation*, ed. Michael Cromartie (Lanham, MD: Rowman & Littlefield, 2005), 9.

12. "The Chicago Declaration of Evangelical Social Concern," November 25, 1973, *The Center for Public Justice*, http://www.cpjustice.org/stories/storyReader$928.

13. Nathan Glazer, "Fundamentalism: A Defensive Offensive," in *Piety & Politics: Evangelicals and Fundamentalists Confront the World*, ed. Richard Neuhaus and Michael Cromartie (Washington, D.C.: Ethics and Public Policy Center, 1987), 250.

14. James Dobson, "The Values Test," *New York Times*, October 4, 2007, http://www.nytimes.com/2007/10/04/opinion/04dobson.html.

15. Editorial, "FOF's James Dobson: A Rogue Elephant in the GOP 'Big Tent,'" *Church & State*, vol. 51, no. 3, March 1998.

16. Robert Sullivan, "An Army of the Faithful," *New York Times*, April 25, 1993, http://www.nytimes.com/1993/04/25/magazine/an-army-of-the-faithful.html?pagewanted=1.

17. Robert D. Putnam, *Bowling Alone: The Collapse and Revival of American Community* (New York: Simon & Schuster, 2001), 162.

18. Cited in John Tracy Ellis, *American Catholicism*, 2nd edition, revised (Chicago: University of Chicago Press, 1969), 151.

19. Christian Coalition direct mailing, quoted in Jon A. Shields, *The Democratic Virtues of the Christian Right* (Princeton: Princeton University Press, 2009), 48.

20. Carl F. H. Henry, *No Longer Exiles: The Religious Right in American Politics*, ed. Michael Cromartie (Washington, D.C.: Ethics and Public Policy Center, 1993), 76.

21. Jerry Falwell, *Listen, America!* (Garden City, NY: Doubleday, 1980), 29.

22. "Transcript of Pat Robertson's Interview with Jerry Falwell," originally aired on *The 700 Club*, September 13, 2001, http://www.commondreams.org/news2001/0917-03.htm.

23. The Associated Press, "Iran: Fashion That Moves the Earth," *New York Times*, April 19, 2010, http://www.nytimes.com/2010/04/20/world/middleeast/20briefs-Iran.html.

24. Daniel Burke, "Religious People Make Better Citizens, Study Says," The Pew Forum on Religion & Public Life, May 13, 2009, http://pewforum.org/Religion-News/Religious-people-make-better-citizens-study-says.aspx.

CHAPTER THREE

A New Approach

Today we are in a transitional moment. One model of religious engagement, embodied by the religious right (and in its own way by the religious left), is fading. A new one will eventually emerge in its place. To understand what that may look like, it's useful to return briefly to where we are.

Two things stand out. First, we are seeing wholesale leadership changes. Within the Christian right, a generation has either passed away (D. James Kennedy, Jerry Falwell) or has seen its influence fading (James Dobson, Pat Robertson). In short, the people who helped bring Christians into the political process after decades of self-imposed exile are themselves now passing from the scene.

Second, as we have already seen, many Christians have turned against the brand of politics practiced by some in positions of leadership. On the basis of extensive polling data, the researchers David Kinnaman and Gabe Lyons conclude,

> Many believers, including faith segments we define as evangelicals and other born-again Christians . . . perceive the politics of conservative Christians as a challenge facing the country. [A 2007 poll] showed that one-sixth of born-again Christians (17 percent) firmly embrace this viewpoint, while nearly half have some degree of concern.[1]

The media have exacerbated this situation. Showcasing individuals more likely to indulge in provocative than in measured speech, they have helped caricature evangelical Christians as a whole and have confirmed the prejudices of large segments of the non-religious population. We say "caricature" because portraying a small handful of cases as representative of the evangelical world is unfair. Ordinary evangelicals, as Christian Smith concludes from a three-year national study, "live in different worlds and have different experiences, concerns, thoughts, and goals than those [whom] journalists and scholars often take to be their leaders."[2]

The question is, What are the "concerns, thoughts, and goals" of today's conservative Christians? And what sort of political engagement might draw their renewed support?

A LOOK AT THE LANDSCAPE

When it comes to conservative Christian attitudes toward social policy, a couple of things seem to be happening at once: on some issues evangelicals are holding on to traditional views while on others they are undergoing an evolution.

To start with the former category, most evangelicals remain strongly attached to a "culture-of-life" agenda; abortion is still the most consistently important issue to them. In a 2008 BeliefNet poll, almost 64 percent of evangelicals over the age of sixty said ending abortion was very important, while, strikingly, the figure for those aged twenty-nine and younger was even higher.[3] According to a Pew poll, almost 70 percent of evangelicals under age thirty consider themselves pro-life.

If opposition to abortion continues to be a high priority among evangelicals, opposition to same-sex marriage remains similarly strong, running to 80 percent among white evangelicals. At the same time, though, the issue of homosexuality per se is receding in salience, especially among the millennial generation. This follows a broader trend in America. "More and more sensible evangelicals would say that we're all sexually confused and that we're all sexually broken. And that therefore tolerance is in order," states Michael Cromartie of the Ethics and Public Policy Center. "But tolerance doesn't mean approval. Across the board, people don't want marriage to be redefined, legally."[4]

This brings us to the attitudes that are in flux. Over the last decade, a number of new issues have gained prominence for evangelicals. Increasing numbers, for example, show concern for environmental issues—"creation care," in the lexicon of some Christians—although few regard this as a top challenge facing the nation and only around a quarter (27 percent) firmly believe that global warming is happening.[5] Among evangelical leaders, there has also been an increased focus on human-rights issues like religious persecution and genocide, as well as "social justice" issues like poverty, AIDS, and conditions in the continent of Africa.

During the Clinton administration, a bipartisan group of religious leaders spoke out in behalf of greater religious freedom around the world. During the Bush presidency, attention was focused on genocide in Sudan. And evangelicals worked with people of other faiths to pass the president's Emergency Plan for AIDS Relief, an unprecedented American commitment to combat the global HIV/AIDS epidemic. These causes are still far from top-tier concerns for most evangelicals, but they are now a part of the conversation.

Another issue that has emerged in the last two years is likely to become increasingly significant. Evangelicals clearly perceive the growing size and reach of the federal government as a threat to our economy and prosperity. By nature, evangelicals tend to be individualistic and skeptical of big government, which they associate with a more liberal political and social agenda. But added to this now is a cultural aspect, coalescing around a different axis from what we are used to. The Tea Party movement comprises millions of Christians whose energy derives primarily from fiscal concerns that are expressed largely in cultural terms.

Younger evangelicals are especially suspicious of big government, indeed of large institutions in general. A generation raised on the Internet and that has come of age with YouTube, TIVO, and WebMD is not inclined to place much faith in centralized control or management by bureaucracy. Though younger evangelicals embrace the social obligation to redress suffering and injustice, they tend to favor means other than large government programs.

What we are seeing, then, is not so much a turnaround—the evangelical movement's long-standing concern with an issue such as abortion is not receding—as an expansion of the agenda. "Evangelicalism is in a time of major self-examination," says John Yates, rector of the Falls Church. "Certainly there is a sensitivity to be living out the social implications of the gospel that is much broader than even ten years ago."[6] While the populist "blue-collar evangelicals"—those who belong to the more fundamentalist and Pentecostal wing of the movement—still identify with the older religious-right model, younger, upper-middle-class, and more highly educated evangelicals are, in the words of Mark Rodgers, "pursuing alternative forms of engagement as well as issues not traditionally associated with the religious right."[7]

And where is the contemporary evangelical movement looking for leadership? Increasingly, it is identified with voices like that of Rick Warren, the senior pastor of Saddleback Church and author of the runaway bestselling book *The Purpose Driven Life.* During the 2008 presidential campaign, Warren hosted a conversation between John McCain and Barack Obama and won praise for his skillful, fair-minded interviewing of both men. Warren is an example of both the shift in tone and the shift in priorities that we have been describing. A social conservative, he and his wife, Kay, have devoted an enormous amount of time and effort to help heal the suffering on the African continent.

"The New Testament says the church is the body of Christ," Warren has declared, "but for the last 100 years, the hands and feet have been amputated, and the church has just been a mouth. And mostly, it's been known for what it's against. . . . I'm so tired of Christians being known for what they're against."[8]

Another influential figure who has emerged on the evangelical scene during the last decade is Timothy J. Keller. Known for his persuasive, culturally informed, and literary sermons (he's been called "Manhattan's leading evangelist" by the *New York Times*), Keller is the senior pastor at Redeemer Presbyterian Church in New York City and the bestselling author of *The Reason for God.*

Neither Warren nor Keller is a political leader per se, and Keller is largely apolitical.[9] But their manner and style—non-abrasive, culturally sophisticated, theologically conservative, in search of common ground where possible—is evidently what more and more evangelicals would like to see in those who speak out on political issues.

Just as potential new leaders are emerging from outside the framework of the older religious right, existing organizations are also detaching themselves from the model that has prevailed for several decades. At Focus on the Family, James Dobson, a key figure in America's "culture wars," has been replaced by Jim Daly, who is much less confrontational in his approach. "I cannot be Dr. Dobson," Daly told the *Denver Post*. "He's black and white—a scientist. That's a good thing. He's provided clarity for the culture. For me, it's more about having a conversation with people."[10] Elsewhere Daly added, "I think the difference [from Dobson's approach] will be the dialogue, engaging people who may disagree in a more aggressive way—in a good way."[11]

And we see a similar change among younger Christians who, though no less concerned than their elders with the moral underpinnings of our culture, feel more at home in our society. As they do not feel under siege, or marginalized, a culturally defensive posture holds no attraction for them. Like many other evangelicals, they want to remain engaged in public affairs, but we detect no groundswell for separatism or full-scale withdrawal.

WHAT THE FUTURE MAY HOLD

Broadly speaking, an increasing number of evangelicals want their brand of politics to be less partisan and bitter than in the past—and than recent American politics in general—as well as more high-minded and more firmly rooted in principles. They want their leaders to display a lighter touch, a less desperate and anxious spirit, a more gracious tone. In short, they seem to be looking for a politics that is both moral and civil. *And*, they are thirsting for more serious Christian reflection on human society and the human person —on first principles.

What does this mean for politicians looking for the votes, not to mention the allegiance, of evangelical Christians? Here it may be helpful to have a brief look at recent voting patterns.

According to John Green, the "basic structure of faith-based politics in the United States was very similar in 2008" to what it was in 2004. Thus, among nearly every religious group, Barack Obama received at least as much support as did the 2004 Democratic nominee, John Kerry.[12] Among Protestants overall, Obama's total was up five points from the 2004 figure of 40 percent.

But the similarity also hides some important differences. Obama and the Democrats made their largest gains among religious groups that can be described as minorities in ethnic, racial, or religious terms (prominently including Hispanic Catholics and Hispanic Protestants). By contrast, among regular worship-attending white evangelical Protestants—i.e., the core of Christian conservatism—

more than eight out of ten continued to vote Republican, making this the single strongest Republican bloc. John McCain, who in fact inspired relatively little passion and even some antipathy in evangelical voters, carried 73 percent of white evangelicals/born-agains, down only six percentage points from the numbers who voted for George W. Bush in 2004.[13]

What about attitudes toward the parties themselves? In 2009, Americans continued to view Republicans as friendlier to religion than Democrats. In fact, the figures reveal a noticeable setback for the Democrats. In mid-2008, 15 percent of Americans described the Democratic party as positively unfriendly toward religion; by the end of last year, that figure had risen to 22 percent.[14]

Nor is it only Republicans and white evangelical Protestants who believe the Democrats' stance toward religion has grown more critical; the same is true of independents as well as moderate and conservative Democrats, and the same is also true of nearly all major religious groups. Only among black Protestants (45 percent) and the religiously unaffiliated (36 percent) do the Democrats score fairly well on the index of friendliness toward religion.

Obviously, in winning over today's and possibly also tomorrow's evangelicals, the Democrats have the steepest hill to climb. Although Barack Obama and his party had a chance to make significant headway with evangelical Christians in the aftermath of the 2008 election, he and they have declined the opportunity. To many, the Democrats appear to be no less hostile than ever to a pro-life agenda and no less opposed to religion playing an important role in our common life. So long as this continues to be the case, there will be a relatively low cap on the support Democrats can hope to gain from this population.

For its part, the GOP still has a number of built-in advantages when it comes to evangelical Christians, simply by virtue of its placement on the policy spectrum. It is a morally conservative party, and it does not appear to be instinctively distrustful of people of faith.

But Republicans also have obstacles to overcome. In particular, the party needs to develop a more sophisticated approach to religion and public life. The old appeals, the old formulations, and the old ways are largely spent; in many cases, invoking them creates more resentment than support. Symbolic gestures—here, some vocal support for impossible-to-pass constitutional amendments; there, a red-meat speech on social values—are not enough. This is particularly true of gestures perceived as advancing merely partisan ends and deepening social divisions. Many Christian leaders—pastors and seminarians, leaders of parachurch organizations, and public intellectuals—feel their witness was hurt because their faith was perceived as an appendage of a political party, as a cog in a party machine.

The Christian political movement is changing and maturing. The younger generation feels alienated by leading figures on both the right and the left. Along with so many of their elders, they are looking for something deeper and something better.

NOTES

1. David Kinnaman and Gabe Lyons, *Un-Christian* (Grand Rapids: Baker Books, 2009), 156.

2. Christian Smith, *Christian America? What Evangelicals Really Want* (Berkeley: University of California Press, 2002), 8.

3. Steven Waldman, comment on "Abortion vs. Homosexuality: The Evangelical Age Gap," BeliefNet Blog, comment posted on July 8, 2008, http://blog.beliefnet.com/stevenwaldman/2008/07/abortion-vs-homosexuality-the.html.

4. Lisa Miller, "Love Thy (Gay) Neighbor," *Newsweek*, October 13, 2007, http://www.newsweek.com/2007/10/13/love-thy-gay-neighbor.html.

5. The Barna Group, "Evangelicals Go 'Green' with Caution," September 22, 2008, http://www.barna.org/barna-update/article/13-culture/23-evangelicals-go-qgreenq-with-caution.

6. Peter Wehner, "Among Evangelicals, a Transformation," *National Review*, December 31, 2007, http://nrd.nationalreview.com/article/?q= ZTRmZTE2OTc3YjlmMGQ4YzBlYTYxODYzMmQ4OTdiMDY.

7. Kinnaman and Lyons, *Un-Christian*, 177.

8. Paul Nussbaum, "The Purpose-Driven Pastor," *Philadelphia Inquirer*, January 12, 2006, http://www.philly.com/mld/inquirer/living/ religion/13573441.htm.

9. Rick Warren was involved in Proposition 8 in California, banning same-sex marriage. He became a visible figure during that campaign and his involvement in it, combined with some of his comments about homosexuality, garnered disapproval among critics of the Proposition.

10. Electra Draper, "Focus on the Family's New CEO Shifts Perspectives," *Denver Post*, June 13, 2009, http://www.denverpost.com/commented/ ci_12581442.

11. Jacqueline L. Salmon, "Dobson's Successor Praises Obama, Looks for Common Ground," *Washington Post*, June 22, 2009, http://newsweek. washingtonpost.com/onfaith/godingovernment/2009/06/by_jacqueline _l_salmon_below.html.

12. Pew Forum on Religion & Public Life, "Event Transcript: A Post-Election Look at Religious Voters in the 2008 Election," Ethics and Public Policy Centerr, http://www.eppc.org/programs/ecl/publications/ program ID.31, pubID. 3726/pub_detail.asp. Of those who attended worship services regularly, more than four in ten people, 43 percent, voted for Obama, while Kerry carried 39 percent of that group.

13. Pew Forum on Religion & Public Life, "How the Faithful Voted," November 5, 2008, http://pewforum.org/Politics-and-Elections/How-the-Faithful-Voted.aspx. Around 60 percent of evangelicals are regular worship attendees.

14. Pew Forum on Religion & Public Life, "GOP Seen as Friendlier to Religion than Democrats," December 1, 2009, http://pewforum.org/ Politics-and-Elections/GOP-Seen-as-Friendlier-To-Religion-Than-Democrats.aspx.

CHAPTER FOUR

The Morality
of Human Rights

In thinking about the future shape of social and political engagement by Christian conservatives, it is helpful to differentiate
between "domestic" and "foreign" concerns. If we begin in this
chapter with the realm of the international, it is because the stakes
there often seem highest.

For good reason: issues of war and peace, human rights and
genocide, extreme poverty and pandemics have massive human
consequences and, therefore, unavoidably moral dimensions. A political theology that fails to reach beyond national borders would be
narrow indeed. And yet, nowhere do the views of Christians appear more diverse, even disjointed, than when it comes to foreign
affairs—and to the formulation of the nation's foreign policy by
American presidents impelled by explicitly Christian beliefs.

In the World War I era, Woodrow Wilson brought explicitly
Christian assumptions to his brand of foreign-policy liberalism.
He was an idealist about America's global role—making the world

safe for democracy, was the way he put it—and a moralist about Europe's failures in this regard. No wonder British Prime Minister David Lloyd George observed of him: "I really think that at first the idealistic President regarded himself as a missionary whose function was to rescue the poor European heathen from their age-long worship of false and fiery gods."[1]

Was Wilson successful? His first secretary of state was the prominent evangelical William Jennings Bryan, whom we have already met. In 1913 and 1914, Bryan negotiated thirty "cooling-off treaties" in which disputing nations agreed to submit their disagreements to binding international arbitration and wait a year before taking any unilateral action. Almost immediately, the agreements proved to be useless scraps of paper. As Wilson moved America toward war in Europe, Bryan resigned in protest.

Skip forward many decades to President Jimmy Carter, himself an evangelical and one who brought a similar religious framework to foreign affairs. Carter placed conspicuous rhetorical emphasis on human rights and the resolution of conflict. "There is no nobler calling on this earth than the seeking for peace," he said. "For it is the reason which caused the Bible to say that peacemakers shall be called sons of God."[2] America, Carter proclaimed, would be "the champion of peace, freedom, and democracy, of human rights, environmental quality, and the alleviation of suffering."[3] His record too was mixed, as rhetoric and action often failed to achieve a meaningful match.

Indeed, this may be why the main influence of evangelical Christians on more recent foreign policy has been to support conservative presidents with notably more muscular approaches to the international scene. In the final decade of the Cold War, evangelicals were strong supporters of President Ronald Reagan's military buildup and rollback strategy against the Soviet Union. During George W. Bush's presidency, they remained some of the most reliable supporters of the Iraq war even after other groups had lost faith in the enterprise.

And yet, despite the very serious foreign-policy disagreements between a Jimmy Carter and a George W. Bush, both were informed by Christian convictions. Is it then possible to discern a number of common themes, at least at a general level, that characterize the views of those two leaders and of others who have likewise appealed to their faith in envisioning America's global role?

We believe so. Such leaders have consistently seen America's role as broader than maintaining the global balance of power or the management of existing international relations. They have asserted an American exceptionalism: a calling, rooted in the philosophy of the founding, to defend and exemplify certain ideals in the world. Their foreign-policy approaches have been active, visionary, and moral. They have spoken frequently of human rights and human dignity. They have rejected the aspirations of empire, but embraced the idea of global responsibility. Both Carter and Bush, for example, were fond of justifying American policies with the biblical verse, "To whom much is given, of him much is required."[4]

This moral conception of America's international role has not always been consistently or successfully applied. Wilson was fully capable of brutalizing Mexico, Carter of coddling dictators. Idealism can be rigid, blundering, or even counterproductive. But exceptionalism and moralism are distinctively Christian contributions in American foreign policy. They can be abused and misunderstood. Yet in the history of the last century, they have been irreplaceable. We believe that an active and practical concern for human rights is among the most important elements of a Christian political theology. And as other philosophical foundations for the idea of human rights weaken and fail, we believe that the religious foundation for human rights will assume even greater importance.

A MORAL GUIDEPOST

The role of religion in international affairs cannot be considered apart from the European Holocaust of the late 1930s and 1940s—the most important moral and political event of modern times. Since the gates of the death camps opened in 1945, the Holocaust has served an essential symbolic purpose. It is the bottom of every slippery slope, the nightmare that wakes us suddenly to the stakes of politics.

In his masterful book *The Years of Extermination*, the historian Saul Friedlander deploys page after page of accumulating detail to reveal the scale and horror of this event: the racial purity laws, the economic indignities, the despairing suicides, the liquidation of the disabled, the digging up of Jewish graves in cemeteries, the deportations, the ghettos, the shootings in batch after batch, the pits of corpses, the emptied orphanages, the naked, terrified walk to the gas chamber, the bodies reduced to smoke and ash. One observer called it "the rule of death in all its majesty"—to the tune of six million Jewish victims.

After the 1939 invasion of Poland, the Special Purpose Operation Group of the Germany army was charged with terrorizing the Jewish population. "The choice victims were Orthodox Jews," Friedlander writes,

> given their distinctive looks and attire. They were shot at; they were compelled to smear feces on each other; they had to jump, crawl, sing, clean excrement with prayer shawls, dance around the bonfires of burning Torah scrolls. They were whipped, forced to eat pork, or had Jewish stars carved on their foreheads. The "beard game" was the most popular entertainment of all: Beards and sidelocks were shorn, plucked, torn, set afire, hacked off with or without parts of skin, cheeks, or jaws, to the amusement of a usually large audience of cheering soldiers.[5]

It is easy to forget how shocking the events of the Holocaust, whose full extent was revealed only after the end of the war in 1945, were to the conscience of the world. The institutions of the modern state—bureaucracy, mass suasion, military power—had been harnessed to the purposes of sadism and mass murder. The Holocaust indicted a highly sophisticated and educated European society —along with the very idea that higher education and cultural sophistication would act as brakes on evil. It indicted other nations that did little, even after the crimes became obvious. It indicted German Christians who were often indifferent or complicit. For some, it even indicted God, who seemed uncaring on a distant throne.

But in many ways the response to the Holocaust was also hopeful. Following the horrors of World War I, the general reaction had been cynicism and disillusionment. Following the greater horrors of World War II, the general reaction was quite idealistic. The victorious Allies instituted a new order of justice and human rights. The Tokyo Tribunals and the Nuremberg Trials were moral as well as legal enterprises. U.S. Supreme Court Chief Justice Robert Jackson, chief counsel for the prosecution at Nuremberg, said of those on trial that the prosecution would not seek convictions "for mere technical or incidental transgressions of international convention. We charge guilt . . . that involves moral as well as legal wrong . . . it is their abnormal and inhuman conduct that brings them to this bar."[6]

The moral response to the Holocaust found equally strong expression in the United Nation's Universal Declaration of Human Rights, which spoke of "inherent dignity" and "equal and inalienable rights." There were many American influences on this document, ranging from the Declaration of Independence to President Franklin Roosevelt's Four Freedoms. But the theory was simple: the Nazis not only lost, they were evil. Their vision of nation, race, and culture would be replaced by an assertion of universal human rights and dignity.

UNIVERSAL HUMAN RIGHTS UNDER CHALLENGE

It was, however, more an assertion than an argument. The French Catholic philosopher Jacques Maritain, who was involved in the discussions surrounding the Universal Declaration, observed: "We agree on these rights, providing we are not asked why. With the 'why,' the dispute begins."[7] Indeed, even as the Universal Declaration was adopted in 1948, challenges were gathering. Three nations abstained from supporting the document: the Soviet Union, Saudi Arabia, and South Africa (which was then run by a white, racist regime). The arguments they made are still heard sixty years later, and for that reason are very much worth considering and answering.

There are three main objections to the idea of universal human rights. First, authoritarian regimes often claim a cultural exception. The philosophy of universal human rights, in their view, is merely an expression, and a tool, of Western culture—a form of ideological colonialism. The pursuit of the Soviet "new man," or of "Asian values," is just as valid. Many autocratic elites in Africa today make a similar argument, identifying the issue of Western-style human rights with colonial arrogance.

The problem with this objection should be obvious: it is fundamentally self-interested, and designed to protect the guilty. A few years ago, the Interfaith Project on Human Rights concluded, "To date, governmental claims that culture justifies deviating from human-rights standards have been made exclusively by states that have demonstrably bad human-rights records."[8] Elites who claim to speak for their culture are actually speaking for themselves and their interests—which often stand in stark contrast to the best traditions of their own culture. There was nothing inherently or admirably Chinese about the Cultural Revolution. There is nothing nobly African about Robert Mugabe's brutal rule.

Indeed, the opposite proposition can be argued—namely, that by deferring to claims of cultural exceptionalism advanced by autocrats, we participate in a kind of colonialism, or what Richard Just of the *New Republic* has called "internal colonialism."[9] These elites treat their people very much the same way that colonial elites once did, or worse. "Is it a consolation for the victims," Just asks, "that their oppression does not come from the West?"[10]

This is an issue on which international institutions themselves are schizophrenic, or worse. The United Nations, for example, was founded on a belief in universal human rights, but also on the principle of state sovereignty and nonintervention. The two are often in tension. The UN asserts the "responsibility to protect": the duty of member nations to rescue the citizens of other nations from crimes against humanity.

Yet the Security Council and Human Rights Council are dominated by nation-states that make such interventions difficult or impossible. From this contradiction there issues paralysis—punctuated by the gang-up of autocratic members of the (misnamed) Human Rights Council against Western countries and most egregiously against the democratic state of Israel. That other nations, many of them home to barbaric and lawless regimes, obsessively excoriate Israel, one of the most admirable and estimable nations on earth—under the banner of human rights, no less—is a travesty and a moral scandal of the highest order.

A second objection to universal human rights has come from religion—and in the first instance not only from Muslim-majority countries but also from the then-Calvinists of South Africa. There, the ruling Afrikaners invoked the Old Testament to justify their vision of white rule. Regarding black Africans as the children of Ham and less than human, they resisted the judgment by outsiders of their religious beliefs, which were merged with their view of the state.

The problem here was similar to the problem with autocratic cultural exceptionalism. Claiming to speak for their religious tradition, South Africa's leaders were actually speaking for a single, distorted version of that tradition. The same can be said of today's militant Islam. The Taliban may assert that stoning a mother to death for adultery before a cheering crowd at a soccer stadium is an authentic application of Islamic law, but the claim is as easily refuted by serious analysis of the Islamic tradition as apartheid was refuted by serious analysis of Christian tradition. Once again, exceptionalism of this kind is revealed as the view of a self-protective elite.

The third objection has come from within the West itself, and specifically from philosophical relativism. Tracing the varieties of relativism is beyond our scope here, but it has become common, particularly in academia, to deny that human beings have natures that can be separated from their cultural circumstances or that are answerable to a source of authority from outside those circumstances. Some, speaking more bluntly, say that we are merely the result of our biochemical processes and our particular environment. That being the case, we have only our own cultural consensus on what constitutes human rights—for us. Not only is it next to impossible to define a universal set of such rights, but we also have no good justification for telling other societies, or for that matter even our own children, why they should hold to our particular consensus.

These trends have opened up a tension at the heart of modern liberalism, whose greatest achievements have lain precisely in the realm of human rights: the Seneca Falls Declaration, which demanded women's rights; the Thirteenth Amendment, which abolished slavery; the Nineteenth Amendment, securing the right to vote; the Civil Rights Act of 1964, which outlawed segregation. Yet just as our bloody modern history has made the idea of human rights more essential than ever, academic liberalism has become infected by the doctrines of relativism and multiculturalism that render any moral commitment to human rights unexplainable.

Or at least unexplained. In the words of Thomas Franck of New York University's School of Law, "Leaders of liberal societies everywhere—political, intellectual, industrial—are being challenged to defend values and clarify distinctions they may have assumed were self-evident."[11] A few have nevertheless tried. Some academics speak of "common morality" or "the common understanding" or "the standard secular account." Martha Nussbaum of the University of Chicago asserts, "It seems to be a mark of the human being to care for others and feel disturbance when bad things happen to them."[12]

But others, with some justice, call this a species of bluffing. Here is Michael Perry of Northwestern University: "If it were a mark of every human being to care for every other human being . . . the 'why' question would be merely academic. But because very many human beings—indeed, perhaps most human beings—have not in the past cared for, nor do they today care for, every human being, the question is both practical and urgent: Why is the good of every human being an end worth pursuing in its own right?"[13]

Indeed, philosophers have tried for centuries to formulate a firm, secular theory of human rights. None has gained broad, much less universal, assent, and none seems equal to the challenge of Nietzsche: if God is really dead, what is to stop the radical, destructive human will? As for the contemporary academic discussion sketched above, much of it seems hung on a peg in midair. What truly marks human beings is the tendency to care for self, family, clan, tribe, race, religion, nation. To care for every human being would appear to require a moral law. To sacrifice for the rights of other human beings—merely because they are human beings—would appear to require a holy law.

ENTER RELIGION

The contribution of religion to this debate is narrow but essential. Why narrow? Because, as we observed earlier, most of the important elements of religious doctrine—eschatology, ecclesiology, soteriology—don't have a direct bearing on politics. Why essential?

Because there is one element of religious teaching with direct and unavoidable public consequence. This is anthropology: that is, beliefs about human worth, human nature, and human destiny.

Why do human beings possess inherent value? The philosophers have their own questioned and questionable theories. Jews and Christians have an answer. They believe that men and women are created equal in worth, in the image of God. They believe in a human nature, which demands human rights.

The belief, then, is crystal clear. Historically, however, the transformation of institutional Christianity into a defender of human rights has been slow and halting. For many centuries of Western history, the Christian church vied and jostled for political power along with other interests, pursuing a tribal agenda at the expense of Jews, heretics, and "infidels." But in our own time, that has dramatically changed.

The Catholic Church, once a reactionary opponent of individualism and modernity, is now one of the leading advocates of universal human rights. Here is Pope John Paul II:

> It must certainly be admitted that man always exists in a culture, but it must also be admitted that man is not exhaustively defined by the same culture. . . . The very progress of cultures demonstrates that there is something in man which transcends those cultures. This "something" is precisely human nature: this nature is itself the measure of culture and the condition ensuring that man does not become the prisoner of any of his cultures, but asserts his personal dignity by living in accordance with the profound truth of his being.[14]

Evangelicals have begun to make the same transition—or, more accurately, to make it again. At its roots in the eighteenth and nineteenth centuries, evangelicalism applied a Christian vision of human nature to the abolition of slavery and the relief of urban poverty. The early twentieth century brought cultural retreat. The twenty-first century is seeing a flowering of social engagement on issues related to human rights. During the last decade, evangelicals were involved in passing the International Religious Freedom Act, which raised the profile of freedom of conscience in the conduct of American policy; in passing the Trafficking Victims Protection Act and the North Korean Human Rights Act; in pushing for a resolution to Sudan's devastating north-south civil war; in promoting global efforts against AIDS and malaria.

This Christian ideal of human dignity is important precisely because it transcends culture. It has proven its ability to stand in judgment of many cultures, including our own. The theologian Max Stackhouse calls this "one of the greatest revolutions in the history of humanity." Christianity, he says, led to the "formation of institutions differentiated from both familial, tribal, and ethnic identity as well as from political authority."[15] Religious people have a unique ability to stand outside the prison of culture and call attention to a set of universal ideals. In other words, they can represent, in the kingdoms of this world, the values of another Kingdom.

PUTTING BELIEF INTO ACTION

The task is not easy. Nor is a belief in universal ideals an excuse for arrogance. Nations with more traditional cultures than ours have some reasonable disagreements with the West, on matters both substantive and procedural. A belief in human rights and dignity does not need to travel with, for instance, all the baggage of the sexual revolution; a headscarf is not a human-rights violation. Human-rights reformers in other cultures will work and speak from within their own traditions. Still, every culture, thank God, has within it some tradition of respect for others to build upon.

The task of applying ideals is especially difficult because governing is itself often difficult. The proclamation of a human right does not directly determine a public policy. It is one thing to say, "The people of Darfur should be rescued from violence." But those in government have responsibilities beyond moral clarity. What are the prospects that an intervention would be successful? What might be its unintended consequences? What other responsible goals would be undermined by a diversion of resources? Even great nations have limited power. Given a serious violation of human rights, there are often several morally permissible courses. Prudence in making a choice is also a virtue.

For all the complexity, however, certain principles are clear. In the Christian view of human rights, human beings stand at the center of concern. This means that the sovereignty of the state is not absolute. The claims of human dignity are universal. Human worth is not determined by nationality, and the responsibility to care for human dignity is not bounded by borders. This belief requires the rejection of a simplistic foreign-policy "realism": the notion that the internal conduct of foreign regimes is irrelevant to the conduct of American policy. America promotes human rights and human dignity for a realistic reason—because brutal nations tend to be aggressive nations. But we also promote human rights because there are moral as well as legal wrongs, and because some conduct is abnormal and inhuman.

It is sometimes charged that moral arguments in foreign policy are always a deceptive cover for self-serving national interest. But this view is wrong in theory and in fact. One historical example is the abolition of the slave trade.

The trade had been developed and expanded by the most enlightened and culturally progressive nations of Europe. Investors over the years included Isaac Newton, John Locke, the British royal family, and the Church of England. There was great profit and little stigma in this mainstream form of commerce in the nineteenth century. Yet, within a hundred years, slavery was illegal everywhere in the Americas.

For decades, historians have attempted to give an impersonal, "structural" explanation for the change: namely, that the end of the slave trade and of slavery somehow served the needs of rising industrial capitalism, which depended on free labor. One leading historian, David Brion Davis of Yale University, offers a different view. The slave trade, he says, was itself a "modern and economically successful system" that "fueled the first great wave of globalization." From Caribbean sugar plantations, to Peruvian mines, to American tobacco plantations, slavery was essential to the economic development of the New World, and to the consolidation of European strategic gains against the Islamic world. Thus, Davis argues, slavery "was not doomed by some implacable force of historical progress."[16]

What then? Davis gives the lion's share of credit to the abolitionists. "Without them I think that from the 1780s to the 1880s very little would have been done." Abolitionists not only conducted a successful public campaign against slavery, they created a new way of political thinking. In their view, says Davis, "providence could reveal itself only through a new human ability—the ability of an enlightened and righteous public to control the course of events."[17]

The abolitionists demonstrated that religion and conscience can be a force for good in the world, that the darkest instincts and destructive interests of humanity can sometimes be overcome, and that foreign-policy idealism is possible and powerful. Davis concludes,

> While there is little evidence that human nature has changed for the better over the past two millennia, a few historical events, like Britain's abolition of its extremely profitable slave trade, suggest that human history has also been something more than an endless contest of greed and power.[18]

We ourselves were privileged to witness another historical example. In 2003, while we were both in the White House, George W. Bush announced the President's Emergency Plan for AIDS Relief

(PEPFAR), the largest program in history to fight a single disease. The plan included $15 billion over five years to promote prevention, treatment, and compassionate care, mainly in Africa. Many were skeptical that large-scale AIDS treatment was even possible in the developing world. But a recent study at the University of British Columbia finds that PEPFAR saved 1.2 million lives in just its first three years.

There was little political benefit for the Bush administration to take such action—and little expectation in the world that it would. The proposal came out of an internal White House policy process that reflected the moral convictions of the president and his senior advisers. To be sure, a simple determination of American interests might have suggested *some* action in this area—the stability of portions of Africa was being undermined by AIDS—but interest alone would never have led to such boldness. In Rwanda five or six years ago, about 4 percent of people who needed AIDS drugs got them. Today, that figure is about 94 percent. Similar results are seen across the continent. It is one reason we two will never be cynical about the ability of government to serve the cause of human dignity, or about the power of a single moral leader to bend history in the direction of justice.

THE RESPONSIBILITY OF FAITH

The idea of human rights is in crisis. "If, as I suspect," says Michael Perry, "there exists no plausible nonreligious ground for the morality of human rights, then the growing marginalization of religious belief in . . . many liberal democracies . . . may leave those societies bereft of the intellectual resources to sustain the morality of human rights."[19] For this reason, the religious foundation for human rights cannot be ignored or dismissed. Whatever the value of secular, philosophical approaches, many who sustain and expand human rights activism are likely to be motivated by faith.

For the same reason, people of faith have a tremendous responsibility. Their activism has never been more important to the welfare of millions. Much about the future justice of the world will be decided by the successes and failures of their conscience.

The Holocaust Memorial Museum in Washington, D.C. preserves the artifacts of history's greatest crime. Around the museum, etched in the walls, are passages from the Torah along with statements of Holocaust survivors and American presidents. But the quotation above the entrance to the museum is not from Scripture or a Holocaust witness. It reads, "We hold these truths to be self-evident, that all men are created equal, that they are endowed by their Creator with certain unalienable rights, that among these are life, liberty and the pursuit of happiness." The Declaration of Independence was accorded this place of prominence because it is, for all time, the negation of Nazism, the check on willful, lawless power, the definition of an idealism that makes us human.

The Declaration would make little sense without the word "Creator": the God who both grants our rights and calls us to protect the rights of others.

NOTES

1. Paul F. Bollwer, *Presidential Anecdotes* (New York: Oxford University Press, 1996), 220.

2. D. Jason Berggren and Nicol C. Rae, "Jimmy Carter and George W. Bush: Faith, Foreign Policy, and an Evangelical Presidential Style," *Presidential Studies Quarterly* 36, no. 4 (December 2006): 617.

3. Ibid.

4. Luke 12:48.

5. Saul Friedlander, *The Years of Extermination: Nazi Germany and the Jews, 1939–1945* (New York: Harper Perennial, 2008), 27–28.

6. Chief of Counsel Robert H. Jackson, Opening Statement for the Prosecution, Nuremberg Trials (November 21, 1945), reprinted in *II Trial of the Major War Criminals Before the International Military Tribunal 102* (1947).

7. Jacques Maritain, *Man and the State* (Washington, D.C.: CUA Press, 1998), 77.

8. Quoted in Max Stackhouse, "Sources of Basic Human Rights Ideas: A Christian Perspective" (paper presented at the University of Chicago Divinity School, Chicago, Illinois, January 27, 2003), http://pewforum. org/Politics-and-Elections/Sources-of-Basic-Human-Rights-Ideas-A-Christian-Perspective.aspx.

9. Richard Just, "We Can't Just Do Nothing: Can a Liberal Be Both Opposed to Imperialism and Devoted to Human Rights?", *New Republic*, August 27, 2009, http://www.tnr.com/article/books-and-arts/we-cant-just-do-nothing?page=0,3.

10. Ibid.

11. Thomas Franck, "Are Human Rights Universal?", *Foreign Affairs* (January/February 2001), http://www.foreignaffairs.com/author/thomas-m-franck.

12. Martha Nussbaum, "Skepticism about Practical Reason in Literature and the Law," *Harvard Law Review* 744 (1994).

13. Michael Perry, *The Idea of Human Rights* (New York: Oxford University Press, 2000), 60.

14. Pope John Paul II, "*Veritatis splendor*," August 6, 1993, http://www.vatican.va/holy_father/john_paul_ii/encyclicals/documents/hf_jp-ii_enc_06081993_veritatis-splendor_en.html.

15. Max Stackhouse, "Sources of Basic Human Rights Ideas: A Christian Perspective" (paper presented at the University of Chicago Divinity School, Chicago, Illinois, January 27, 2003), http://pewforum.org/Politics-and-Elections/Sources-of-Basic-Human-Rights-Ideas-A-Christian-Perspective.aspx.

16. Michael Gerson, "Unchained by Idealism," *Washington Post*, June 20, 2007, http://www.washingtonpost.com/wp-dyn/content/article/2007/06/19/AR2007061901737.html.

17. Ibid.

18. Ibid.

19. Michael Perry, "The Morality of Human Rights," *Commonweal*, July 14, 2006, 16.

CHAPTER FIVE

The Role *and* Purpose
of the State

Having worked in the White House during two wars, the worst attack on the American homeland in our history, the worst natural disaster in our history, and a recession, we have some appreciation for how the rush of events and the demand for action can push aside the ability to focus on fundamental questions and first principles. Public service can be fulfilling and energizing; it can also be frantic and exhausting. The pressure is unceasing, the chance for mistakes and errors ever present. Sometimes it is difficult to think straight, let alone to think deeply.

But thinking deeply is what those who care about politics need to do. Just as we would not want to build a house without a blueprint, we should not debate issues or decide policy matters without a proper framework of ideas. What *ought* to be the role of government in our lives as Christians? God willed the state, as Edmund Burke put it; but what does He want the state to achieve?

This is hardly a new question. Some of the greatest Christian minds—from St. Paul, St. Augustine, and Thomas Aquinas to Jonathan Edwards, Richard Hooker, and Abraham Kuyper; from John Courtney Murray and Reinhold Niebuhr to Martin Luther King Jr. and John Paul II—have built an impressive tradition of interpretation around this question. As they have taught us, politics in its best sense is not about power for its own sake; it is about the ends we hope to achieve through the use of power.

THE TRANQUILITY OF ORDER

There are, we believe, four categories—order, justice, virtue, and prosperity—that can help Christians think through the proper role of government in our lives. They are not exhaustive, and our discussion of them is hardly definitive. But, based on our own work, experience, and reflections over the years, we will try to inject these somewhat abstract concepts with concrete meaning.

Perhaps the best place to begin is with what St. Augustine referred to as *tranquillitas ordinis*, or "the tranquility of order." For him, this had both a negative and a positive connotation: negative in the sense that order was necessary to prevent anarchy, and positive in the sense that order creates the conditions for many other good things.[1]

Order is, in fact, the first responsibility of government. "Among the many objects to which a wise and free people find it necessary to direct their attention," John Jay wrote in *Federalist No. 3*, "that of providing for their safety seems to be the first."

Order is the *sine qua non*, the necessary precondition. Without it, we can hardly expect justice, prosperity, or virtue to flourish. And order cannot be achieved without government. It is an instrument sanctioned by God.

St. Paul understood this quite well. In Romans 13:4, he writes: "For [a ruler] is God's servant to do you good. But if you do wrong, be afraid, for he does not bear the sword for nothing. He is God's servant, an agent of wrath to bring punishment on the wrongdoer."

St. Paul is saying two things here. First, rulers are God's servants. This builds on verses in the Hebrew Bible, including Isaiah 45:1, where Cyrus, a foreign emperor, is called "his anointed" because God has designated him to carry out a divine commission. Second, rulers exist for the benefit of society and in order to protect the general public—when necessary by punishing wrongdoers.

Few have understood this Pauline point as well as the American founders. To take just one example: in 1786 and 1787, Massachusetts experienced an armed uprising led by Daniel Shays, a veteran of the American Revolution. In an effort to prevent the foreclosure of farms as a result of high interest rates and taxes, ex-Revolutionary War soldiers had taken up arms against a state government too weak to put an end to the rebellion on its own. Finally, a volunteer army had to disperse the rebels.

This episode stirred fears of anarchy among the founders and helped to convince them that the existing Articles of Confederation were an insufficient bulwark of government. Exceeding their original mandate, which was to revise the Articles of Confederation, the delegates in Philadelphia replaced them with the Constitution, one of whose core purposes was, in the words of the preamble, to "insure domestic tranquility."

But the aim of government is not *simply* order. After all, totalitarian regimes specialize in establishing order, which they accomplish by systematically violating civil and human rights—that is, to borrow a vivid image from George Orwell, by means of a jackboot stomping on a human face. Rather, the proper aim is order established under the rule of law and respectful of lines and limits. And this leads to a question that in one form or another has occupied the minds of philosophers and political thinkers for centuries. Is it indeed possible to institute order while respecting basic rights, or is an oppressive state the only real alternative to chaos?

The Christian view of human nature—which not coincidentally was the view of the American founders as well—argues for the former position, and for a middle ground between anarchy and the chains of despotism. On the one hand, Christian anthropology believes people are flawed and fallen, that sin is a congenital and inescapable condition, and that perfection or anything close to it is beyond our reach. On the other hand, it recognizes that human beings, created in the image of God, are capable of acts of reason and responsibility, love and loyalty, compassion and courage. The vast majority of us are neither angels nor devils.

A wise government, constructed around a true view of human nature, thus creates the conditions necessary to allow the great mass of the people to live well and to flourish, to enjoy both order and liberty, to live under the protection of the state without being suffocated by it.

THE THREAT OF DISORDER

Among the threats to domestic order, crime surely ranks high. The worst consequences of crime are visited on its victims, in the violence directed against innocent people, in the death, pain, and loss that often accompany criminal acts.

But crime has other collateral effects as well. When crime is rampant, people live in fear. They are afraid to go to school or to work, afraid to shop or to play. The sense of security and community is destroyed. And those who suffer disproportionately are the poor and the weak. "Where the deviant rule," Professor John J. DiIulio Jr. has written, "conservatives can forget about the magic of enterprise zones and liberals can forget about the promise of new social welfare measures."[2]

Crime can provoke other effects as well: feelings of revenge and vigilantism among citizens who feel they cannot rely on the state to meet its most basic obligation and who sometimes decide to take justice into their own hands. Civil libertarians, anxious to protect the rights of criminals, sometimes forget that, if crime is allowed to go unchecked for prolonged periods of time, the public may insist that civil liberties themselves be rolled back. Social anarchy eventually gives rise to authoritarianism. "No society," wrote the constitutional law expert Alexander Bickel, "will long remain open and attached to peaceable politics and the decent and controlled use of public force if fear for personal safety is the ordinary experience of large numbers."[3]

When crime is prevalent, moreover, our laws are made a mockery. What are decent people to think, how are they to behave, if there is no punishment for wrongdoing? The moral point is put well by Stanley C. Brubaker:

> We should understand punishment as a kind of mirror image of praise. If praise expresses gratitude and approbation, punishment expresses resentment and reprobation. If praise expresses what the political community admires and what unites it, punishment expresses what the community condemns and what threatens it. Punishment, like praise, publicly expresses our determinations of what people deserve.[4]

"BEARING THE SWORD"

Crime, then, ought to concern all responsible citizens. And in response to it, Christians need to strive for the right balance between imposing order and respecting civil and human rights. While this is not the place for a comprehensive analysis of the subject, we do have some thoughts on what responsible anti-crime policies would entail.

There can be little doubt that the stunning drop in crime that America has witnessed since the early 1990s—some types of crime have been reduced to levels we haven't seen since the mid-1960s—is due in large part to a policy revolution in law enforcement. Innovators like then-Mayor Rudolph Giuliani in New York City and his police chief William Bratton pursued a zero-tolerance approach to crime that quickly became a model for other cities and states.

Policing improved, crime statistics were processed faster, criminal patterns were identified more effectively, and incarceration rates rose—all of which furthered the twin goals of intervention and prevention. In programs like Philadelphia's Youth Violence Reduction Partnership, an array of urban agencies, working together, drove down homicide rates in the most violent areas by focusing on youths most at risk of killing or being killed.

There was a theory here, known as the "broken windows" concept of law enforcement. What Giuliani and other successful lawmakers did, with remarkable skill, was to apply ideas and methods developed by Professors James Q. Wilson and George L. Kelling, who in the early 1980s observed that allowing a broken window to remain unrepaired was a sign of neighborhood indifference. It invited more broken windows, eventually turning the area into a magnet for criminals seeking a hassle-free environment in which to pursue their aims.

The deeper point Wilson and Kelling were making is that public disorder—dilapidated and abandoned buildings, graffiti and litter, pornography shops, and a generally run-down appearance—is evidence of a permissive moral environment. It is a signal that no one cares. As Plato framed the same point, it suggests "corruption in [the] very souls" of those charged with *keeping* order.[5]

In city after city, we have seen how enforcing good laws has allowed public space to be regained, order and civility restored, and civic life revivified. Progress against crime required government coercion, but it has been carried out in a manner far from capricious or draconian. Criminals have rights, from lawyers to trials to an appeals process. Third parties arbitrate the process. Punishment is meted out to the guilty, but they are protected against the violent wrath of victims and their families and can avail themselves of the promise of rehabilitation. Our laws treat even the worst criminals with the kind of decency and respect that they never demonstrated to their victims. That is a sign of a decent and humane civilization, and one consistent with a Christian ethic.

Crime is the result of evil that exists within the human heart. Government is charged with restraining such evil—and when it acts intelligently and comprehensively, it can fulfill both its biblical and its secular mandate.

"JUSTICE IS THE END OF GOVERNMENT"

"Justice is the end of government," James Madison wrote in *Federalist No. 51*. But what is the meaning of justice?

This is another question that has been discussed and debated for millennia, ever since Abraham pleaded for justice on Sodom's behalf to God. Justice has been variously defined as the quality of being impartial and fair, the equal treatment of equals, and living in accordance with the natural law and the divine plan. It implies integrity in dealing with others and conforming our lives to facts and to truth.

In Plato's *Republic*, a debate between Thrasymachus and Socrates focuses on the meaning of justice. To the cynical Thrasymachus, "a just man always has the worst of it"—for the simple reason that "justice" is not something intrisically good but only a pretty word for what is in the interest of the stronger party. Therefore, he argues, let us be honest, prefer injustice, and live accordingly. Might makes right.

Socrates utterly rejects this argument, insisting that justice is not only an intrinsic good but is central to human happiness and a well-ordered soul. "Just men are superior in character and intelligence and more effective in action," Socrates says. "Indeed without justice men cannot act together at all."

The views of Socrates find some support in the Scriptures. "Follow justice and justice alone, so that you may live and possess the land the Lord your God is giving you," the Hebrew Bible teaches us. "The Lord loves righteousness and justice; the earth is full of his unfailing love," we read in the book of Psalms.

What Judaism and Christianity have added to our understanding of justice—their distinctive and lasting contribution—is the importance of caring for the weak, the disadvantaged, and the oppressed. "I know that the Lord secures justice for the poor and upholds the cause of the needy," David writes in the Psalms. "The righteous care about justice for the poor, but the wicked have no such concern," according to Proverbs. "Cursed is the man who withholds justice from the alien, the fatherless or the widow," is how Deuteronomy puts it.

Jesus Himself tells us in Matthew, "Truly I say to you, to the extent that you did it to one of these brothers of Mine, even the least of them, you did it to Me" (NASB). And for those who do not aid the stranger and the person who is hungry and thirsty, who does not clothe the destitute or visit the sick and those in prison, Christ's words are haunting. "Truly I say to you, to the extent that you did not do it to one of the least of these, you did not do it to Me."

This is a central teaching of Christianity. At its core is the belief that everyone, no matter at what station or in what season of life, has inherent dignity and rights. These are not only a private concern but also a public one. Throughout Scripture, rulers are judged by whether the weak and the disadvantaged in society are cared for or exploited. The attitude of Thrasymachus and Nietzsche—that might makes right and that the strong should rule the weak—is foreign to Judaism and biblical Christianity.

How does this view of justice relate to particular areas of life where the powers of government are involved? We shall look at economics shortly; here, we turn to the issue of abortion.

LIFE VERSUS CHOICE

What is the moral significance and proper legal status of life in its earliest stages? What are the claims and rights of early unborn life? Thoughtful people disagree on the answers to these questions. In the "life versus choice" debate, we place ourselves, with most evangelical Christians, firmly in the camp of the culture of life. And we base our position on both biology and justice.

When it comes to abortion, we freely admit that some individual cases are very complicated. These include pregnancies that are the products of rape or incest, or that involve medical threats to the life of the mother. We are also enormously sympathetic to those, faced with an unwanted pregnancy or with the birth of a special-needs child, whose lives are about to be turned upside down and who consider abortion to be the only way out. We cannot pretend that the answers are neat, easy, or obvious.

Still, a few principles are clear. First, unborn children are in fact human. The fetus is genetically complete and distinct. Unless it perishes due to natural causes or violent outside intervention, it will become a child, not a giraffe. It is a human being at a very early stage of development, just as a ninety-nine-year-old is a human being at a very late and frail state of development.

Second, eliminating a defenseless human being is a deeply problematic act.[6] When it happens on a routine basis—on the order of more than three thousand abortions per day—it becomes a direct challenge to a society's commitment to justice.

As a practical matter, we accept the fact that the earliest abortions will probably not be legally restricted any time soon. Any effort to preventing early-term abortions is therefore likely to lie in the realm of persuasion rather than law. That said, incremental progress and further revelations about the humanity of unborn children can alter social attitudes over time. In fact, inroads have been made already. After reaching a national high of over 1.6 million in 1990, the number of abortions performed annually in the U.S. has dropped to fewer than 1.3 million, a low not seen since the Supreme Court's 1973 decision legalizing the practice in *Roe v. Wade*. And the American consensus is certainly more pro-life than current practice would suggest. America is becoming more, not less, pro-life.[7]

Two decades ago, many pro-life spokesmen changed their rhetorical tactics and began to choose their fights more carefully. Throughout much of the '90s, the debate became colored by the clear-cut issue of partial-birth abortion, which, although not settled legislatively until 2003, helped to create greater social sympathy for a moderately pro-life position. Also contributing to the re-thinking was the more widespread use of sonogram technology, which enables would-be parents to see the developing child and its human form at a very early stage. All in all, not only has the public discussion of abortion been profoundly transformed, but younger Americans, as we have previously discussed, seem to have moved the furthest on this issue and this trend seems likely to continue.

Yet the abortion debate goes beyond practicalities to fundamental issues of justice.

In medical ethics, there is a philosophical divide between utilitarianism, the belief in the greatest good for the greatest number, and the belief in the inherent human dignity of every individual. At bottom, the utilitarian approach is an assertion of the power of the strong over the weak; it treats human beings as means rather than as ends. By contrast, the belief in human dignity is rooted in the Jewish-Christian tradition of regarding the protection of innocent lives as one of the primary purposes of a just society.

Given the increasing technological control that human beings have over their own nature, this conflict has important implications for the future. A utilitarian society will be dramatically different from, and dramatically less humane than, a society that honors the principle of human dignity. We know which one will be better for the weak. And we know that to stand for justice when the prevailing winds are gusting in the direction of individualism and utilitarianism is a worthwhile enterprise. The greatest achievement of the religious right is to have engaged in this enterprise, year in and year out, patient in tribulation and undeterred by Supreme Court rulings and attacks from elite opinion.

"It was once said that the moral test of government," remarked the great liberal champion Hubert Humphrey, "is how that government treats those who are in the dawn of life, the children; those who are in the twilight of life, the elderly; and those who are in the shadows of life, the sick, the needy and the handicapped." These are beautiful and evocative words, and they set a worthy standard for the state. Unborn children are at the dawn of life, and a moral test of our government, and of anyone thinking about or acting in government, is how they are treated.

"SUPPLEMENT YOUR FAITH WITH VIRTUE"

For the ancient Greeks, happiness was defined as the soul acting in accordance with virtue. This is a concept consistent with the teaching of the Scriptures. Here is St. Paul in his letter to the Philippians: "Finally, brothers, whatever is true, whatever is honorable, whatever is just, whatever is pure, whatever is lovely, whatever is commendable, if there is any excellence, if there is anything worthy of praise, think about these things" (ESV).

And St. Peter: "For this very reason, make every effort to supplement your faith with virtue, and virtue with knowledge" (ESV).

This is a Christian calling, and it is also a democratic one. As James Madison put it in *Federalist Paper No. 55*:

> As there is a degree of depravity in mankind which requires a certain degree of circumspection and distrust, so there are other qualities in human nature which justify a certain position of esteem and confidence. Republican government presupposes the existence of these qualities in a higher degree than any other form.

The need for virtue is greatest in free societies because they depend on self-government, on citizens who govern themselves and their passions and who lead decent, law-abiding lives. And this in turn is one of the reasons that the founders, almost to a person, regarded religion as a foundation stone for democracy.

"THE MOST IMPORTANT
SOCIAL ACHIEVEMENT OF MANKIND"

The main responsibility for inculcating virtue rests with the family, which esteemed academics James Q. Wilson and the late Richard J. Herrnstein called "the most important social achievement of mankind."[8] From our faith perspective, it is the God-given task of parents to teach their children about right and wrong, restraint and self-control, diligence and discipline, sympathy and fairness, loyalty and hard work. If they fail in these efforts, the ramifications can be enormous, both for the child and for society more broadly. No federal agency or government program, no matter how good, can replace a mother and father.

This does not require us to idealize parents. As fathers ourselves, we are all too familiar with our shortcomings in this respect. But even flawed parents occupy a unique place in the hearts and lives of their children. That relationship, more than any on earth, is characterized by unconditional love and an unbreakable bond. This means that parents have an unparalleled, if not an unlimited, capacity to nurture children and to shape their character. If they fail, or aren't around, others can and should step into the breach—but the task of character education will be harder, usually much harder, and in some cases very nearly impossible.

A second source of character-formation is institutions like schools, church and other houses of worship, neighborhoods, voluntary associations, and community organizations. Important are not the institutions per se but the individuals who comprise them. Teachers, pastors, rabbis, coaches, Scout leaders—all are influential forces in the lives of children.

What every parent wishes is for their children to be surrounded by individuals of good character and high moral purpose. The examples set by athletes and entertainers, by the movies and television shows children watch and by the songs they listen to, influence for good or for ill the efforts by parents and society at large. "What we have loved, others will love, and we will teach them how," is the way the nineteenth-century poet William Wordsworth put it. In this case, the "we" includes parents and the community of adults in the lives of children.

CHARACTER-SHAPING INSTITUTIONS AND THE STATE

The role of government in the formation of human character tends to be indirect and limited, certainly when compared with other governmental initiatives like building roads and enforcing free trade agreements. This is as it should be. There is simply no way that an entity like government—often impersonal, bureaucratic, unfeeling, and unresponsive—can compete with, let alone replace, parents. Devotion and sacrificial love are qualities we associate with mothers and fathers, not with the Department of Motor Vehicles or the FTC.

Authoritarian and totalitarian regimes accord primacy to the state in almost every regard. The American tradition views the role of government as far more circumscribed, designed to create space for civil society to grow and to flourish. But from time to time, statecraft engages in soulcraft as well. Just as attitudes, mores, and manners shape laws, laws shape attitudes, mores, and manners. Beyond that, laws and government policies can affirm, or weaken, character-forming institutions like the family.

An example is a social-welfare program like Aid to Families with Dependent Children (AFDC). Not only did this program fail to improve the condition of the poor, which was its explicit purpose, it created greater dependency on government and encouraged out-of-wedlock births. Between 1960 and 1990, the percentage of children relying on AFDC increased from 3.5 to almost 13 percent, while the out-of-wedlock birth rates increased by more than 400 percent.[9] This happened despite the fact that total social spending (in constant dollars) by the federal government increased by a factor of five and a half.[10]

What explains the explosion in these social pathologies? As usual, the answer lies in a mix of factors, including a substantial shift in American social attitudes. But surely one explanation is that government actually created an incentive for the poor to become dependent on welfare and to form fatherless families. By law, we issued checks to poor, unmarried women so long as they (a) did not work and (b) were not married to an employed male. The more children a woman had, the greater the subsidy she would receive. Before it was reformed in 1996, our federal welfare program served as a life-support system for fatherless families.

Or take the issue of divorce.[11] In 1970, Governor Ronald Reagan of California signed into law the nation's first "no fault" divorce law. Within just seven years, all but three states had repealed fault grounds for divorce. This amounted to a revolution in social policy. In less than a decade, the entire legal divorce structure was fundamentally changed. Not surprisingly, how Americans viewed marriage underwent a profound shift as well. After carefully analyzing the data, William Galston, a top domestic adviser to President Bill Clinton, concluded that the switch in the law "led to a measurable increase in the divorce rate."[12] We now know that, for most children, divorce has a shattering emotional and developmental effect.

Then there is the issue of same-sex marriage—something unthinkable two generations ago but now legal in five states. (Four additional states, plus the District of Columbia, recognize marriages by same-sex couples legally performed elsewhere.) Legal endorsements eventually translate into widespread social acceptance. That is precisely what is happening in this instance. Whatever one thinks about same-sex marriage, we are in the midst of a sea-change in attitudes toward it, with support at record highs.[13]

The effects on the institution of marriage itself are impossible to know as yet. Some believe—and this is our predisposition—that same-sex marriage will redefine marriage in a harmful way, prying it from its biological, religious, and cultural roots and further weakening its authority; others believe marriage will accommodate gays just as it has other changes in the past, creating hardly a ripple in the long term; still others argue that, by bonding gays into committed, stable relationships, same-sex marriage will prove to be a profoundly traditionalizing act.[14]

It is simply too early to say what broader effect legalized same-sex marriage may have—but it is reasonable to assume that other institutions, including schools and churches, will increasingly be affected by the shift from a policy of social tolerance for gays to government-endorsed sanction of gay marriage. If such marriage is deemed to be a civil right—and if opponents are therefore deemed to be the equivalent of modern-day segregationists—churches may eventually be compelled to act in a way that complies with the spirit and letter of "anti-discrimination" law rather than with orthodox Christian teaching.

Here then are three issues related to families—out-of-wedlock births, divorce, and gay marriage—in which governmental policies have exercised varying degrees of impact. And this is only part of the story. Government also has a large role in determining the quality of our schools, and of other institutions engaged in molding what Jefferson referred to as our "morals" and "faculties." We have our views on these matters as well. But perhaps we have said enough to underline the main point, which is the radical inadequacy of a public discourse oriented, as ours now is, toward individual rights.

People, as Aristotle taught, are social beings at their core. We find fulfillment in association with others, and the formation of human character thus depends on the strength and well-being of key social institutions. In a thousand different ways—large and small, subtle and crude—the acts of government can promote or undermine these value-shaping institutions, thereby influencing whether the American republic will indeed be a "regime of virtue,"15 committed to human and moral excellence.

PROSPERITY

The issues of economics, wealth, and prosperity are often given short shrift among Christians. It strikes many of them, including conservative evangelical Christians, as inhabiting a lower order of concern.

Others feel slightly embarrassed to speak up for wealth-creation, let alone for capitalism. They believe it cuts against the grain of Scripture and the words of Jesus, who after all warned His followers, "It is easier for a camel to go through the eye of a needle than for a rich man to enter the kingdom of God." St. Paul wrote, similarly, that the love of money is the root of numerous evils.

Yet estimable figures in the Bible, like Abraham and Solomon, were wealthy. "Lazy hands make a man poor," according to Proverbs, "but diligent hands bring wealth." Private property is taken for granted in the Hebrew Bible; otherwise, the commandment "Thou shalt not steal" would not have much meaning. Indeed, restitution is required in the case of theft, and biblical injunctions to give away one's wealth—even if taken literally—are clearly to be understood as urgings toward personal charity.16

What a contextual reading of the Bible tells us, it's fair to say, is that wealth can be a snare that we have to be careful to avoid. But so are other things: pride, envy, lust, gluttony, wrath. Our hearts are easily drawn to material things. What Jesus and St. Paul were describing, then, was a *spiritual* temptation, and a very serious and real one; however, neither figure outlined an economic system. Like the Sermon on the Mount, which we discussed in chapter 1, Jesus' words were meant to guide personal behavior, not to establish a political platform.

And so, as is almost always the case when it comes to Christianity and political philosophy, what we are dealing with in regard to economic systems is a prudential calculation, not a matter of church doctrine. Those who insist that Christianity explicitly endorses this or that economic system have planted their flag on treacherous ground. The case for and against capitalism should be made on its merits—and about this, we do have some things to say.

First, no other economic system—not socialism, not autarky, and surely not communism—can compare to capitalism as an engine of economic growth, wealth creation, and human achievement. This in itself should mean a great deal to anyone concerned for the poor and the oppressed.

Capitalism has produced two things that for much of history were regarded as inconceivable: a large middle class and intergenerational wealth-building. In so doing, it has lifted untold numbers of people out of mass poverty and mass misery. What is more, the medical, scientific, and technological advancements that have resulted from capitalism have brought wholeness and healing to countless lives. By contrast, where capitalism has not yet taken root we find destitution, widespread misery and illiteracy, and much early death.

Because of the wealth created by capitalism, charity and generosity are possible. The moral philosopher Adam Smith, who was also the father of modern economics, put it this way: "If our own misery pinches us very severely, we have no leisure to attend to that of our neighbor." Americans, fortunate to be able to attend to their neighbors, gave more than $300 billion to charity last year, to say nothing of the millions of American citizens who volunteer for charitable work.[17] The successes of capitalism make all of this possible.

Free markets also go hand in hand with free societies. Both require government to be limited in its power and reach. Both depend on transparency and accountability. And both trust people to act in ways that advance their self-interest and the interests of society. It is no coincidence that totalitarian governments view capitalism as an unacceptable threat to their authority. To allow people freedom in one realm will lead to another, and then another, threatening a police state with the loss of its grip on power.

The material prosperity generated by capitalism, then, is an indisputable social and moral good.

Yet it is necessary to add that capitalism produces wealth more easily than it produces character. Its ranks include individuals who (being human) can be greedy, careless, and reckless. We are all too familiar with examples of financial fraud and Ponzi schemes, with the manipulation of markets and insider trading, with companies that cut corners in order to make a quick buck.

Which is to say that capitalism, for all its strengths, is hardly self-sufficient or self-sustaining. Like democracy itself, it depends on a citizenry characterized by certain habits of mind and heart: men and women who possess traits like self-discipline, honesty, and sympathy. And so we return once again to the indispensable role played by families, schools, and churches, builders of human character and nurturers of human virtues.

Nor is that the end of the matter. Capitalism is not a natural phenomenon; it is, in fact, a social creation, a product of the state. Laws are its rules. It therefore muddies rather than clarifies the debate to say that we have to choose between government and markets. The relevant question—in this context, the only truly useful question—is not whether the state has a role to play but what the nature of that role ought to be.

In order to properly function, capitalism relies on the state, and specifically on a state that respects the free market without bowing down before it. "Properly understood, the case for capitalism is not a case for license or for laissez-faire," Yuval Levin has written:

> It is a case for national wealth as a moral good; for the interest of the
> mass of consumers as the guide of policy; for clear and uniform
> rules of competition imposed upon all; for letting markets set prices,

letting buyers make choices, and letting producers experiment, innovate, and make what they think they can sell—all while protecting consumers and punishing abuses. It is a case for avoiding concentrations of power, for keeping business and government separate, and for letting those who can meet their own needs do so. It is a case for humility about our ability to know, and therefore about our capacity to do.[18]

Exactly so. In reflecting on the strengths and blessings provided by capitalism, we need to acknowledge its limitations and think about how to deal wisely with them. An irreplaceable engine of growth and progress, it can also, as the Industrial Revolution showed, produce enormous social dislocation. In the inevitable transition from one industry to another, certain people can get run over. This is what Joseph Schumpeter, a great champion of capitalism, called the system's quality of "creative destruction." The role of the state is to help cushion the blows of capitalism and to offer help to those who cannot help themselves.

"There's a growing recognition," Professor Mary Ann Glendon has written, "that human beings do not flourish if the conditions under which we work and raise our families are entirely subject either to the play of market forces or to the will of distant bureaucrats. The search is on for practical alternatives to hardhearted laissez-faire on the one hand and ham-fisted, top-down regulation on the other."[19] That is the mark of a decent and advanced society.

No magic formula can tell Christians what the precise admixture should be between capitalism and the state, between the private and the public sectors. These issues need to be determined through experience, through solutions tried and solutions failed, and with careful regard to facts and circumstances. Entitlement programs like Social Security may well rank as among the most humane social initiatives in American history—but it may be that, because of demographic shifts and new fiscal realities, this program and others need to be fundamentally reformed. Means-testing might make sense at one moment in history, not at another.

The Scriptures, for all their wisdom, offer very little guidance on these matters. What we can take away from them, though, is that an economic system, like an individual life, ought to be judged by the fruit it produces. By that standard, capitalism is, in our estimation, worthy of support, worthy of praise, and worthy of defense.

SKEPTICISM BUT NOT CONTEMPT

In thinking through the large, complicated topic of the role and purpose of the state, a caution is worth noting, perhaps especially for those who share our political views. And that is this: skepticism toward government is often warranted and legitimate; contempt and outright hostility are not. We count ourselves conservatives in the tradition of Edmund Burke, who averred that God instituted government as a means of human improvement.

Government is not simply a necessary evil; so long as it acts within its proper boundaries and in a respectable fashion, it has a positive and constructive role to play in human affairs. Often government at all levels falls short of our expectations. We have certainly seen our share of that in our years of service, especially during the course of events—like the Iraq war in 2006, when America was on the brink of defeat and Iraq was on the brink of civil war—that caused us sleepless nights. At times of trial and failure, those responsible for running government need constructive criticism—admittedly not always as welcome as it should be—and practical suggestions for reform. What they don't need are attacks on government's very legitimacy.

What Christians can best provide are the moral categories and a moral lens—a framework for thinking *about* and thinking *through*—by which policymakers, like the rest of us, can judge the questions before them. However incompletely, we have tried to sketch such a framework here.

NOTES

1. See George Weigel, *Tranquillitas Ordinis: The Present Failure and Future Promise of American Catholic Thought on War and Peace* (New York: Oxford University Press, 1987), 31; and St. Augustine, *City of God*, chapters 11–13, trans. Gerald G. Walsh, S. J.; Demetrius B. Zema, S. J.; Grace Monahan, O.Su.U; and Daniel J. Honan (Garden City, NY: Image Books, 1950).

2. John J. DiIulio, "The Value of Prisons," *Wall Street Journal*, May 13, 1992.

3. Alexander M. Bickel, "Crime, the Courts and the Old Nixon," *New Republic*, June 15, 1968, 8.

4. Stanley C. Brubaker, "In Praise of Punishment," *The Public Interest*, no. 97, fall 1989, 46.

5. *The Republic of Plato*, trans. with introduction and notes by Francis MacDonald Cornford (New York & London: Oxford University Press, 1941), 90.

6. Sixty-seven percent of those who have abortions list as the reasons she (a) feels unready for child/responsibility; (b) feels she can't afford the baby; and (c) has all the children she wants/other family responsibilities: http://www.nrlc.org/abortion/facts/reasonsabortions.html.

7. A Gallup Poll conduced in May 2009 found 51 percent of Americans calling themselves "pro-life" on the issue of abortion and 42 percent "pro-choice." This is the first time a majority of U.S. adults have identified themselves as pro-life since Gallup began asking this question fifteen years ago. See Lydia Saad, "More Americans 'Pro-Life' than 'Pro-Choice' for First Time," Gallup, May 15, 2009: http://www.gallup.com/poll/118399/more-americans-pro-life-than-pro-choice-first-time.aspx.

8. James Q. Wilson and Richard J. Herrnstein, *Crime & Human Nature: The Definitive Study of the Causes of Crime* (New York: Free Press, 1985), 524.

9. William J. Bennett, *The Index of Leading Cultural Indicators: Facts and Figures on the State of American Society* (New York: Touchstone, 1994), 64.

10. Ibid., 66.

11. See William J. Bennet's *The Broken Hearth: Reversing the Moral Collapse of the American Family* (New York: Doubleday, 2001), chapter 5.

12. Paul A. Nakonenzy, Robert D. Shull, and Joseph Lee Rogers, "The Effect of No-Fault Divorce Law on the Divorce Rate Across the 50 States and Its Relation to Income, Education, and Religiosity," *Journal of Marriage and Family*, vol. 57, no. 2 (May 1995), 485.

13. Earlier this year a Gallup Poll showed 53 percent of Americans do not believe same-sex marriage should be recognized as valid by law, while 44

percent believe it should. In 2009, 57 percent of Americans stated gay marriage should not be legal, while 40 percent said the opposite. In the mid-1990s, the gap between support and opposition for same-sex marriage was 33 points. See http://www.gallup.com/poll/135764/americans-acceptance-gay-relations-crosses-threshold.aspx.

14. For a thoroughgoing and thoughtful discussion of same-sex marriage, see William J. Bennett's *The Broken Hearth: Reversing the Moral Collapse of the American Family* (New York: Doubleday, 2001), chapter 4.

15. Leo Strauss, *Liberalism Ancient & Modern* (Chicago: University of Chicago Press, 1968), vi.

16. For a much fuller discussion of capitalism, see Arthur C. Brooks and Peter Wehner, *Wealth and Justice: The Morality of Democratic Capitalism* (Washington, D.C.: AEI Press, 2010).

17. Yuval Levin, "Recovering the Case for Capitalism," *National Affairs*, spring 2010, no. 3, 134.

18. Ibid., 134–35.

19. Mary Ann Glendon, "Beyond the Simple Market-State Dichotomy," *Origins* 26 (May 9, 1996), 797.

CHAPTER SIX

Persuasion *and* *the* Public Square

As evangelicals consider how best to play a role in politics in the twenty-first century, they need to consider not simply *what* they believe on an array of issues but *how* they should articulate and advocate their case and their cause.

In sorting through this matter, the relevant presuppositions are vital. Ours is that persuasion and debate are, in and of themselves, moral goods. There are also utilitarian reasons. In a free society, certain rules govern how we conduct our politics and how we work out our political differences. Unlike in unfree societies, where government proceeds by diktat and decree, we govern ourselves through public arguments, whose goal is to persuade people to believe certain things and vote in certain ways. The ballot is stronger than the bullet, Lincoln said, and we may thank heaven that, for Americans, this choice has long since been made.

But our own convictions on this matter go deeper than merely pragmatic considerations. The importance of persuasion is an essential part of a Christian belief system.

Christ's Great Commission to His followers, after all, was to make disciples of all nations, to teach them His commandments, to spread the "good news" of the gospel. To evangelize means to advocate a cause with the object of making converts, to teach rather than to force, to preach rather than to coerce.

So the very core of preaching and evangelism is based on persuasion, on making compelling public arguments in public settings. And because human beings are created in God's image, they are morally autonomous and free to choose. They are capable of reason, and of being reasoned with. What most separates human beings from animals is a moral conscience, the ability to engage in private and public conversations about the human condition and the well-being of society: conversations that must always leave open the possibility of refinement and readjustment, redefinition and change—and, yes, principled disagreement. The first and foremost goal of an advocate or activist in public life must therefore always be persuasion.

CAN BAD PERSONS MAKE GOOD ARGUMENTS?

There are several pillars upon which effective persuasion rests, beginning with the character of those trying to do the persuading. Aristotle, in his book *Rhetoric*, writes, "There are three things, apart from demonstrative proofs, which inspire belief—namely, sagacity, high character, and good will.... If a person is thought to command them all, he will be deserving of credit in the eyes of his audience."[1]

Aristotle's point is that the integrity of individuals cannot be separated from their arguments. We are all far less inclined to listen to the case for fidelity from a serial adulterer, the case for responsible drinking from a practicing alcoholic, or the case for honesty from a chronic liar. Bad character and bad behavior can discredit good arguments.

Of course, this is not the whole story. Arguments should ultimately be judged on their merits. Loyalty isn't any less a virtue because of disloyalty in the ranks of those who speak out on its behalf. And we need to be careful not to set up a situation in which only perfect individuals are allowed to advance moral arguments. If that becomes the case, then moral arguments will simply vanish. Since sin is a congenital condition, only flawed people can speak out on behalf of moral ideals.

In addition, politicians are not ministers or deacons; the high biblical standards that apply to those holding church office—for example, being the husband of one wife and managing children and households well—are different from those to which we should hold public figures.

Still, we can all agree that, when it comes to the art of persuasion, moral character exerts significant influence. We have all participated in discussions on complicated issues that we cannot fully understand and whose details we don't fully grasp. In those instances we often look to those whom we trust, morally and intellectually, for guidance and ratification. We rightly take their integrity into account when weighing the merits of a particular argument or cause.

This point applies, incidentally, to the American founding. Its success rested not simply on the words and ideals contained in the Declaration of Independence or the Constitution; it also depended on the trust Americans placed in the moral character of George Washington. In 1783, unpaid officers from the Continental Army threatened a military coup to overthrow Congress, which had run out of money. But because of an appeal to them by Washington, whom they revered, the officers voted to give Congress more time to pay them what they were owed.

Washington persuaded the officers to respect the law. Yet his argument won the day because of his character rather than his words. "He was, indeed, in every sense of the words, a wise, a good, and a great man," Jefferson said of him. "Washington errs as other men do, but errs with integrity." Had that not been the case, Americans during the difficult early days of the Republic may well have given up on this "new order for the ages."[2]

We therefore should not view arguments simply in abstract intellectual terms. They are often tethered to the people who advocate them. It's all fairly simple, really: if people cannot trust you, they aren't likely to trust the facts and evidence you marshal on behalf of your cause.

The danger that flawed character will discredit good arguments may be particularly acute for Christians, who are held to an especially high standard of probity. And of course the world is always eager to expose Christians who are moral hypocrites. That is why the Scriptures go to such lengths to instruct followers of Christ to act in a manner that is above reproach, to be blameless in conduct, and to remind Christians that faith without works is dead. "Always be prepared to give an answer to everyone who asks you to give the reason for the hope that you have," St. Peter wrote. "But do this with gentleness and respect, keeping a clear conscience, so that those who speak maliciously against your good behavior in Christ may be ashamed of their slander."

THE ART OF "TRANSLATION"

How, then, to engage in the art of persuasion in a free society, one in which many citizens hold vastly different religious views and some none at all?

Here we can look to St. Paul for some guidance. Upon visiting Athens, according to the book of Acts, Paul was greatly distressed to see that the city was full of idols. "So," we read, "he reasoned in the synagogue with the Jews and the God-fearing Greeks, as well as in the marketplace day by day with those who happened to be there." Then, we are told, a group of Epicurean and Stoic philosophers began to dispute with him. They took him to a meeting on the Areopagus, or Mars Hill.[3]

His interlocutors asked St. Paul about his "new teaching." "You are bringing some strange ideas to our ears," they said, "and we want to know what they mean."

Paul then stood up in the meeting of the Areopagus and said, "Men of Athens! I see that in every way you are very religious. For as I walked around and looked carefully at your objects of worship, I even found an altar with this inscription: TO AN UNKNOWN GOD. Now what you worship as something unknown, I am going to proclaim to you."

St. Paul proceeds to speak about the power and omnipresence of God, as well as God's setting aside a day when He will judge the world with justice.

What can we glean from this encounter? St. Paul, without compromising his message, tailored it to his audience. He spoke to them in Hellenistic rather than Judaic terms, as a philosopher more than as a Christian theologian, in a manner that engaged them rather than repelled them. He relied on common grace rather than on the knowledge and acceptance of Christian doctrine. "I have become all things to all men," he says in the book of Corinthians, "so that by all possible means I might save some."

The Catholic theologian George Weigel calls attention to the apostle's "grammatical ecumenicity," adding,

> If, in such a grand cause, the apostle of the Gentiles could appeal to his audiences through language and images with which they were most familiar—if, to get down to cases, Paul could expropriate an Athenian idol as an instrument for breaking open the Gospel of Christ, the Son of the Living God—then perhaps it is incumbent upon us, working in the far less dramatic vineyards of public policy, to devise means of translating our religious convictions into language and images that can illuminate for all our fellow citizens the

truths of how we ought to live together, as we have come to understand them through faith and reason.[4]

One way this "translating" can be done is through an appeal to
natural law. This is a venerable theory that posits basic rules of conduct that are inherent in human nature, essential to creating a civilized society, and valid and applicable everywhere and always.
Natural law theory asserts that a "moral logic" exists, that it is accessible through human reason and reflection, and that it does not
depend solely on revelation. To set forth, by its lights, the rights
that are due to human beings *qua* human beings is to provide an
ecumenical lens through which to judge individual policies.

Natural law theory is sharply different from the approach embraced by the secular philosophers we examined briefly in chapter
4, who try (and fail) to devise a compelling theory of human rights
while at the same time denying the very existence of human nature.
In fact, natural law theory is most often identified today with the
Roman Catholic Church. Some in the Protestant tradition have rejected it because they fear it minimizes sin. They believe the de-
pravity of man is so deep and complete that God's image in
creation and human nature has been nearly eradicated. Human
reason itself has been irredeemably corrupted, and God's finger-
prints have all but been erased from the human scene.

Yet many of the magisterial Reformers like Luther and Calvin
were believers in natural law.[5] So, arguably, was St. Paul, at least based
on his writings in the first chapter of Romans, where he states,

> The wrath of God is being revealed from heaven against all the god-
> lessness and wickedness of men who suppress the truth by their
> wickedness, since what may be known about God is plain to them,
> because God has made it plain to them. For since the creation of the
> world God's invisible qualities—his eternal power and divine nature
> —have been clearly seen, being understood from what has been
> made, so that men are without excuse.

This interpretive approach has had profound political implications, including in our country. Indeed, an appeal to natural law characterized the work and words of two of history's most eloquent and effective advocates for the American ideal, Abraham Lincoln and the Reverend Dr. Martin Luther King Jr.

Lincoln's and King's lives were committed to reversing two great sins in American history, slavery and segregation, and their appeal to natural law helped them to prevail against those twin evils. In the case of King, one need only consult his 1963 *Letter from Birmingham City Jail*, one of the masterpieces of American political and moral thought.

King was serving a jail sentence for participating in civil rights demonstrations in Birmingham, Alabama. His seven-thousand-word epistle responded to critics who urged him to wage the battle for integration through the courts rather than through acts of non-violent civil disobedience. In the course of his response, King wrote this:

> A just law is a man-made code that squares with the moral law or the law of God. An unjust law is a code that is out of harmony with the moral law. To put it in the terms of Saint Thomas Aquinas, an unjust law is a human law that is not rooted in eternal and natural law. Any law that uplifts human personality is just. Any law that degrades human personality is unjust. All segregation statutes are unjust because segregation distorts the soul and damages the personality. It gives the segregator a false sense of superiority, and the segregated a false sense of inferiority. . . . [S]egregation is not only politically, economically and sociologically unsound, but it is morally wrong and sinful.[6]

A century earlier, a tall, lanky lawyer in Illinois was engaged in a titanic contest that would help shape the meaning and future of the American Republic.

Abraham Lincoln came to fame largely because of his 1858

debates with Stephen Douglas to decide who would represent Illinois in the United States Senate. At the core of their differences was the issue of popular sovereignty.

Douglas, one of the most accomplished orators of his time, did not argue in favor of slavery per se; rather, he argued on behalf of popular will. According to this doctrine, it was up to free citizens in the territories of the United States to decide whether or not to practice slavery. "Trust the people" was Douglas's creed. "The issues between Mr. Lincoln and myself . . . are direct, unequivocal, and irreconcilable," Douglas said. "He goes for uniformity in our domestic institutions, for a war of sections, until one or the other shall be subdued. I go for the great principle of the Kansas-Nebraska Bill—the right of the people to decide for themselves."[7] In this case, remember, the right for people to decide for themselves extended to chattel slavery.

Absolutely not, Lincoln countered. He believed human beings were endowed by their Creator with fundamental rights that were inviolate *regardless* of what popular will said. As for self-government, one could not appeal to that principle while simultaneously denying it to an arbitrary class of human beings. Moreover, Lincoln argued, some things could not be voted up or voted down. The doctrine of popular sovereignty did not, and could not, supersede basic human rights.

In an 1858 speech in Lewistown, Illinois, Lincoln appealed, as he so often did, to our founding document. Quoting from the Declaration of Independence—"We hold these truths to be self evident, that all men are created equal, that they are endowed by their Creator with certain unalienable rights, that among these are life, liberty, and the pursuit of happiness"—he went on to say,

> This was [the founders'] majestic interpretation of the economy of
> the Universe. This was their lofty, and wise, and noble understand-
> ing of the justice of the Creator to His creatures. Yes, gentlemen, to

all His creatures, the whole great family of man. In their enlightened belief, nothing stamped with the Divine image and likeness
was sent into the world to be trodden on, and degraded, and im-
bruted by his fellows.[8]

Both Lincoln and King consciously laid the foundation for promoting human rights and affirming human dignity. In reading
their words and speeches, one cannot help being struck by how
often they used religious symbolism and biblical language to state
their case even as they spoke in a style and parlance that resonated
with all people, not just people of faith.

Lincoln and King treated the public with enormous respect,
employing sophisticated arguments and elevated rhetoric. They re-
turned, time and again, to the founding documents and the ani-
mating principles of the American Republic. They quoted from the
Declaration of Independence, not the Westminster Confession.
They argued from explicit philosophical precepts. And both King
and Lincoln appealed to reason and the common good rather than
revelation and Christian doctrine. They resisted the temptation to
use religious faith and the Scriptures as a partisan club or a political trump card.

Lincoln's and King's words defined two of the great moral
struggles of the nineteenth and twentieth centuries. Their success,
however, was based not only, or even primarily, on their eloquence,
though that certainly didn't hurt. What carried the day for them—
in addition to the force of arms and the force of law—was the logic
and rigor of their arguments and their ability to translate those arguments in a way that moved many human hearts to act. In that respect, and in many others, they have a great deal to teach Christians
in the twenty-first century.

TONE, BEARING, COUNTENANCE

For anyone engaging in the art of persuasion, there are eminently practical reasons for using language that is reasonable, judicious, and sober rather than aggressive, abrasive, and abusive. On the whole, people drawn to a cause like to feel that those representing the cause are both amiable and peaceable.

More important for evangelicals are the injunctions found in the Scriptures, such as this one from the book of Colossians: "Let your conversation be always full of grace, seasoned with salt, so that you may know how to answer everyone." What the apostles call the "peace of Christ" is meant to supplant bitterness and aggression.

A significant dissonance between one's content and one's tone —between the case for human dignity and the language one uses to argue in its behalf—can be discrediting. As the book of James reminds us, fresh water and salt water don't flow from the same source.

None of this precludes rhetorical tough-mindedness. Democracy, after all, was designed for disagreement. Conflicting views are often clarifying. And sometimes a confrontational approach is called for. In his letter to the Galatians, St. Paul confronted St. Peter face-to-face and in front of a group. And Jesus Himself had some withering things to say, especially to the Pharisees. ("You brood of vipers" is fairly vivid language, even by today's standards.) Wit and sarcasm can be powerful instruments when employed in the right way. On the flip side, for some people civility is a synonym for hollowed-out principles, for lukewarm moral commitments, for those who believe nothing and are willing to fight for nothing.

As a general matter, though, personal attacks and extreme charges are inappropriate and ineffective, and in politics they can easily diminish the appeal of a party or a cause. Abraham Lincoln once again framed things in precisely the right way:

> When the conduct of men is designed to be influenced, persuasion, kind, unassuming persuasion, should ever be adopted. It is an old

and true maxim "that a drop of honey catches more flies than a gal-
lon of gall." So with men. If you would win a man to your cause,
first convince him that you are his sincere friend. Therein is a drop
of honey that catches his heart, which, say what you will, is the great
high road to his reason.[9]

Employing the right tone, however, depends on more than utilitarian considerations. More fundamentally it has to do with reflecting a view of human persons and their inherent dignity. It
means treating people with respect and good manners regardless of
the views they might hold.

In taking up these matters we don't for a moment wish to
downplay the difficulty of living up to the standards we recommend. In the arena of politics, not much emphasis is put on what
St. Paul called the fruit of the Spirit—love, joy, peace, patience,
kindness, goodness, faithfulness, gentleness, and self-control. This
is something the two of us have confronted in quite real and practical ways. To put the matter as squarely as we can: How are we to
conduct ourselves as individuals who are intimately involved in
politics and who also proclaim and take seriously their Christian
faith?

During our White House years, we felt a particular challenge
when people attacked President Bush in ways that we deemed to be
reckless, unfair, and *ad hominem*. Prominent politicians of the op-
posing party called him a liar and a loser, a moral coward, a man
who had betrayed his country, and much more. How should we, as
Christians, have dealt with these charges? We knew enough about
politics to know that passions often run high and that it is easy for
debates to become personalized. How, then, were we to stay true
to our convictions and loyal to the president for whom we had
great regard and affection while also maintaining our civility—
and not simply our civility, but a spirit of grace?

A PRIMER FOR CHRISTIAN PERSUADERS

There is no magic formula that anyone can offer up on these matters; much depends on individual facts and circumstances. To know when to hold back and when to fire back often rests with intuition and wisdom. In our experience, though, several considerations are useful in navigating these waters.

- *Maintain self-awareness.* Catholics have a useful term—"occasion of sin." By this they mean a situation that can lead people to stumble and fall. A good way to stay out of trouble is to be aware of what these situations are and, whenever possible, to avoid them. In the political world, one particularly needs to be alert to situations that are likely to evoke strong reactions within oneself, so that one can try to channel those reactions in ways that are useful and constructive, or at least not harmful and damaging.

- *Maintain spiritual grounding.* There is a reason Christians are instructed in Colossians to set their hearts and minds on things above. Doing so has the capacity to transform the human heart, to make believers thankful, and to "put to death" their earthly nature, including anger, rage, malice, and slander.

    Like so many other Christians, we too have been much more likely to lash out at others when our spiritual lives have become enervated, when our faith has been drained of its vitality, and when we have begun to think as citizens of earth instead of as citizens of heaven.

- *Maintain perspective.* One trap for Christians is to begin to believe that they and their cause are indispensable and that God can't accomplish His purposes without them, that "everything that we care about . . . hangs in the balance" of a presidential election, or that "our job is to reclaim America for Christ, whatever the cost."[10]

There's a corrective for that—namely, understanding that God is sovereign and that His purposes will ultimately come to pass. This is not a prescription for passivity or lassitude; in the Hebrew Bible and the New Testament, divine sovereignty and human responsibility are linked. Only when one begins to believe that God isn't sovereign does it become easy to develop an aggressive, anxious, brittle, desperate spirit. The struggle many of us face is to keep from believing that God depends on us instead of the other way around.

• *Maintain community.* For us, as for many others, our spouses are our first and best counselors, the people we go to most often to understand the condition of our own spirit. But there are others—parents and family members, colleagues and friends—to whom we can all turn for advice and guidance, not simply about what we say but about how we are saying it.

For us, it has also been quite helpful to stay in touch with people whom we respect but who don't share our political views. There is an understandable tendency to seek out a community of like-minded individuals who can offer support and encouragement along the way. That is part of what we humans thirst for and rely on. In *The Four Loves,* C. S. Lewis writes that a friendship is born when two people discover they not only share common interests but see the same truth, who stand not face-to-face (as lovers do) but shoulder-to-shoulder.

Still, it's important, especially for those of us involved in politics, to resist the temptation to surround ourselves *exclusively* with like-minded people, those who reinforce our preexisting views and biases. It then becomes easy—much too easy—to caricature and ridicule those with whom we disagree.

In the White House in particular, where you have access to more information than is available to most people and are surrounded by some of the leading experts and brightest individuals in the country, it is quite tempting to think that you and your colleagues are all-wise and your critics are all-foolish. And before long, you can find yourself in an intellectual cul-de-sac. That is a dangerous place to be. We need at least a few people in our orbit who are willing to challenge what we claim and how we claim it.

• *Maintain a spirit of grace and reconciliation.* In some circumstances, the most useful contribution Christians can make in the political sphere is to turn the other cheek, to respond to unwarranted attacks not out of a sense of justice, which may be fully warranted, but out of a spirit of grace and forgiveness.

Such situations are rare; unilateral disarmament in public debate, as in international relations, can all too readily be taken advantage of and turned against one. And in most situations it's not called for. But now and then, forgiving the grievances we have against others can offer a powerful witness to the world.

We saw this in the case of Pope John Paul II who, in 1983, walked into a cell at Rebibbia prison in Rome, took the hand of Mehmet Ali Agca, who had shot and nearly killed him in an assassination attempt, and forgave him. Agca later said, "I am repentant for the attack on the pope."

Another instance: In South Africa, the Truth and Reconciliation Commission, established after the abolition of apartheid, granted amnesty to several hundred individuals who had committed abuses during the apartheid era, on the condition that the crimes were found to be politically (rather than racially) motivated and that there was full disclosure by the person seeking amnesty. The Commission helped move

South Africa away from a spirit of vengeance toward reconciliation.

In American history we have Lincoln's Second Inaugural Address, which—in only 703 words—offered a framework for healing after the carnage of the Civil War. Lincoln spoke about reunification instead of revenge. He spoke about binding up the nation's wounds "with malice toward none, with charity for all."[11] "The address sounded more like a sermon than a state paper," said the great abolitionist Frederick Douglass, who was in the audience for the speech.

Moments like these are rare and difficult to replicate. In the wrong hands, they can come across as contrived and inappropriate. Worse, in the wrong circumstances, they can set back the cause of justice without advancing the cause of reconciliation. Still, Christians should be alert for situations where true grace can lead to true reconciliation, where it can allow people, perhaps for the first time, to view bitter disputes in a gentler light, and where genuine transformation is possible.

AND WHEN YOU LOSE?

Christians have every right, and perhaps even a duty, to bring to the public square their deepest convictions. They should fight for them with wit and skill, with tenacity and persistence.

But it is equally important to accept the fact that in a democracy Christians will sometimes, maybe even often, lose debates, lose elections, and lose power. In some respects the most important question they need to be able to answer is this one: What do you do when your case and your cause don't triumph, when you fight and you lose?

As a general matter we don't recommend losing in any arena, including politics. But we do understand that just as Jesus teaches that the last shall be first, that the poor rather than the rich are blessed, and that the meek shall inherit the earth, sometimes losing in the right way, with the right spirit, can be our greatest public witness. This is when magnanimity and a generosity of spirit are most needed—along with the all-important recognition that, in a democracy, even lost causes can rise again.

NOTES

1. J. E. C. Welldon, trans., *The Rhetoric of Aristotle* (New York: Macmillan, 1885), 113–14.

2. William Eleroy Curtis, *The True Thomas Jefferson* (Philadelphis: B. Lippincott, 1901), 241.

3. *Areopagus* is a Greek word meaning "rock of Ares." Ares was the Greek god of thunder and war. The Roman equivalent was Mars—hence the name "Mars Hill."

4. George Weigel et al., *Disciples & Democracy*, ed. Michael Cromartie (Washington, D.C.: Ethics and Public Policy Center, 1994), 82.

5. Stephen Grabill, *Rediscovering the Natural Law in Reformed Theological Ethics* (Grand Rapids: Eerdmans, 2006); J. Daryl Charles, *Returning to Moral First Things: The Natural-Law Tradition and Its Contemporary Application* (Grand Rapids: Eerdmans, 2008); J. Daryl Charles interview with Ken Myers, *Mars Hill Audio Journal*, volume 93, September/October 2008.

6. J. M. Washington, ed., *A Testament of Hope: The Essential Writings and Speeches of Martin Luther King, Jr.* (San Francisco: HarperCollins, 1986), 293.

7. Abraham Lincoln and Stephen Douglas, *The Lincoln Douglas Debates* (Mineola, NY: Dover Publications, 2004), 23.

8. Mario M. Cuomo and Harold Holzer, eds., *Lincoln on Democracy: His Own Words, with Essays by America's Foremost Civil War Historians* (New York: Fordham University Press, 1990), 122.

9. Abraham Lincoln, "Address to the Washington Temperance Society of Springfield, Illinois," February 22, 1842, in *Lincoln: Speeches, Letters, Miscellaneous Writings/The Lincoln-Douglas Debates* (New York: The Library of America, 1989), 83.

10. Quotes by James Dobson and D. James Kennedy, cited by James D. Hunter, *To Change the World: The Irony, Tragedy & Possibility of Christianity in the Late Modern World* (New York: Oxford University Press, 2010), 127.

11. Ronald C. White Jr., *Lincoln's Greatest Speech: The Second Inaugural* (New York: Simon & Schuster, 2002), 19.

Against Politics, *and* For Politics

It is sometimes said that culture is "upstream" from politics—that what ultimately determines a nation's shape is not its laws but its songs and scholarship, its movies and technological innovations, its novels and newspapers. And there is some truth to this.

Politics usually involves a form of power, exercised through law and taxation. But there are other forms of power in society. The power of beauty and myth. The power of ideas and academic excellence. The power of example and integrity. Ancient Greece was in large part the creation of a blind poet named Homer. The American colonies were the product of a thousand nonconformist sermons.

As we have emphasized throughout this book, the pursuit and exercise of *political* power poses special challenges and dangers to religious believers—ones we have witnessed with our own eyes. The dangers include cultivating bitterness toward opponents, becoming jealous of others with access to power, exploiting or being exploited in the power games of other players. For many

Americans, the spectacle is not only disturbing but discrediting.

A little mental distance from the temptations of politics is a good and necessary thing. In 1951, Prime Minister Winston Churchill offered C. S. Lewis the title of Commander of the British Empire, a high and appropriate distinction. But Lewis refused the honor. "I feel greatly obligated to the Prime Minister," he responded, "and so far as my personal feelings are concerned this honour would be highly agreeable. There are always, however, knaves who say, and fools who believe, that my religious writings are all covert anti-Leftist propaganda, and my appearance in the Honours List would of course strengthen their hands. It is therefore better that I should not appear there."[1] Lewis had higher goals and more urgent priorities than public eminence.

The wrong kind of politics can not only compromise an individual believer but undermine the message of the church itself. Any political movement—even, or particularly, one viewed as virtuous—can become a consuming substitute for faith. And the line is fine between zeal and anger. "I was one of those caught up in the mood and action of the 1960s," writes Sheldon Vanauken in *A Severe Mercy*, a book that touches on his days in the anti-Vietnam war movement:

> Christ, I thought, would surely have me oppose what appeared an unjust war. But the Movement, whatever its ideals, did a good deal of hating. And Christ, gradually, was pushed to the rear: Movement goals, not God, became first, in fact—not only for me but for other Christians involved, including priests. I now think that making God secondary (which in the end is to make Him nothing) is, quite simply, *the* mortal danger in social action, especially in view of the marked intimations of virtue—even arrogant virtue—that often perilously accompany it. Some may avoid this danger, perhaps. But I was not obeying the first and greatest commandment—to love God *first*—nor is it clear that I was obeying the second—to *love* my

neighbour. Hating the oppressors of my neighbour isn't perhaps quite what Christ had in mind.[2]

The same story could just as easily be told about militant activism on the political right.

Politics is not only inherently dangerous; it is inherently difficult. As Reinhold Niebuhr argued, political debates seldom pit light against darkness, despite what the participants may imagine, but instead involve the weighing of relative goods. A military intervention liberates millions while resulting in the death of thousands. An environmental law saves a species or a wilderness for future generations while costing jobs that support families.

In politics, prudence is a higher, rarer virtue than purity. Uncertain judgment calls are both unavoidable and consequential. And those who make such calls can easily fall victim, in Niebuhr's words, to the "insinuation of the interests of the self into even the most ideal enterprises and most universal objectives."

So it is hardly any wonder that, in every generation, some believers conclude that political engagement is not worth the risk and the inevitable cost. We hear those voices once again today. Since culture is upstream from politics, they say, perhaps Christians should relocate to more pleasant territory upriver. Perhaps they should focus more on cultural formation than on political activism. Perhaps they should be content with demonstrating the values of the City of God instead of writing statutes for the City of Man.

IN DEFENSE OF POLITICS

The problem is this: culture is upstream from politics, except in those important cases when politics is upstream from culture.

In April 1963, a group of eight Birmingham clergy members made a famous argument about the limits and dangers of political activism. We read about this moment in chapter 6. In the *Birmingham News*, the clergymen criticized civil rights activism as "unwise and untimely," and urged believers to show patience. Martin Luther King Jr., then in the Birmingham City Jail, began writing a response on the margins of the newspaper. "Frankly," he said, "I have yet to engage in a direct-action campaign that was 'well timed' in the view of those who have not suffered unduly from the disease of segregation."

King's counter-argument was simple and convicting: patience for political injustice comes more easily for those who are not currently experiencing injustice. "Perhaps it is easy," he says,

> for those who have never felt the stinging darts of segregation to say, "Wait." But when you have seen the vicious mobs lynch your mothers and fathers at will and drown your sisters and brothers at whim; when you have seen hate-filled policemen curse, kick and even kill your black brothers and sisters . . . when your first name becomes "nigger," your middle name becomes "boy" (however old you are) and your last name becomes "John," and your wife and mother are never given the respected title "Mrs."; when you are harried by day and haunted by night by the fact that you are a Negro, living constantly at tiptoe stance, never quite knowing what to expect next, and are plagued with inner fears and outer resentments; when you are forever fighting a degenerating sense of "nobodiness"—then you will understand why we find it difficult to wait.

In his *Letter from Birmingham City Jail*, King reserves special criticism for the "white moderate," whom he describes as "more devoted to 'order' than to justice; who prefers a negative peace which is the absence of tension to a positive peace which is the presence of justice . . . who paternalistically believes he can set the timetable for another man's freedom." Instead, King recommends a kind of extremism:

> Was not Jesus an extremist for love: "Love your enemies, bless them that curse you, do good to them that hate you, and pray for them

which despitefully use you, and persecute you." Was not Amos an extremist for justice: "Let justice roll down like waters and righteousness like an ever-flowing stream." Was not Paul an extremist for the Christian gospel: "I bear in my body the marks of the Lord Jesus." Was not Martin Luther an extremist: "Here I stand; I cannot do otherwise, so help me God." And John Bunyan: "I will stay in jail to the end of my days before I make a butchery of my conscience." And Abraham Lincoln: "This nation cannot survive half slave and half free." . . . So the question is not whether we will be extremists, but what kind of extremists we will be. Will we be extremists for hate or for love? Will we be extremists for the preservation of injustice or for the extension of justice?

Of course, not every political issue is as clear or as urgent as the civil rights movement. But it is worth remembering that most evangelicals, at the time, did not find the civil rights struggle particularly clear or urgent, either. "How sad," writes the great Christian pastor John Perkins,

> that so few individuals equally committed to Jesus Christ ever became part of [the civil rights] movement. For what all that political activity needed—and lacked—was spiritual input. Even now, I do not understand why so many evangelicals find a sense of commitment to civil rights and to Jesus Christ an "either-or" proposition. One of the greatest tragedies of the civil rights moment is that evangelicals surrendered their leadership in the movement by default to those with either a bankrupt theology or no theology at all, simply because the vast majority of Bible-believing Christians ignored a great and crucial opportunity in history for genuine ethical action.[3]

In sum, all of the cautions about a politicized faith are true. Niebuhr was correct to urge realism about the world, humility in making grand moral claims, and suspicion toward our own political motives. But Christians, particularly younger Christians, should internalize King's prison letter before accepting Niebuhr's corrective. A distrust of political action—a preference for gradual cultural change—would have left legal segregation in place to this day. Changing a culture of bigotry required both the Civil Rights Act and the Voting Rights Act: coercive measures that created a social expectation of equal treatment and shifted the political balance of power in America. And none of this would have happened without idealism, impatience, and the single-minded pursuit of justice.

THREE CONCLUDING PROPOSITIONS

So we are left, once again, with an unavoidable tension—a necessary complexity. There is danger in a politicized faith, but there is also moral abdication when faith ignores the opportunity for "genuine ethical action." Laws involve coercion. They also create the moral context for a culture, defining the boundaries of the community and the duties we owe our fellow citizens. Laws do more than reflect the pre-existing values of a society; they habituate the ideals and expectations of a society. Even as Christians abandon their political illusions, they cannot avoid their responsibilities as citizens of America and of the City of Man.

We do not claim to have a simple score card of political issues attached to these duties. Individual priorities will and should vary by calling and conviction. But we hope this book leaves the reader with three broad propositions and the arguments supporting them:

- *Politics is the realm of necessity.* At any given moment in a democracy, great issues of justice and morality are at stake. The idea that people of faith can take a sabbatical from politics to collect their thoughts and lick their wounds is a form of irresponsibility. It is, in fact, an idea that could only be embraced by comfortable Christians. If one lives in a neighborhood plagued by poverty, dominated by gangs, and served by failing schools, there is no sabbatical from the failures of politics. Getting drug dealers off the corner and teaching children the basics of reading and math are at least as important as long-term cultural change, and certainly more urgent. If one lives in a foreign country without medicines for AIDS, malaria, tuberculosis, or ruled by a cruel dictator, the current policy priorities of the American people and its government matter greatly. Retreating from the cause of justice, even temporarily, is only conceivable for those who have few needs for justice themselves.

A little political maturity is thus in order. In the last few decades, Christians have often done politics poorly. So do most other groups in our democracy. The answer is to do politics better. Political engagement is not a luxury. The fighting of raging fires requires not contemplation but a fire extinguisher. Urgency can involve errors, and these should be admitted and corrected. But, as G. K. Chesterton said, "Even a bad shot is dignified when he accepts a duel."

• *Politics is the realm of hope and possibility.* In the late 1990s, Paul Weyrich, a prominent leader of the religious right, circulated a public letter declaring that America was "caught up in a cultural collapse of historic proportions, a collapse so great that it simply overwhelms politics." America was descending into "something approaching barbarism." People of faith, Weyrich concluded, should adopt a "strategy of separation." "We need some sort of quarantine."

But something unexpected happened on the way to American cultural collapse. A number of reformers in cities and state governments demonstrated that at least some of our cultural decay was the result not of bad values but of failed policy. Better policies dramatically reduced violent crime rates, cut teenage drug use, ended welfare dependency, encouraged dignified work, and improved performance in many low-income schools. Cultural fatalism was simply not justified.

Problems that may seem intractable at one moment— violence and disorder, harmful and reckless conduct—can yield, and yield quickly, to the right policies and to a determined citizenry. Far from being discredited by recent history, politics has shown a remarkable ability to improve lives. This would be a sad and ironic time to dismiss or devalue the political enterprise.

- *Politics can be the realm of nobility.* At its best, politics is about the right ordering of our lives together. It cannot be unimportant, because justice is never unimportant. Political rhetoric and ideals can raise the moral sights of a nation and point men and women to responsibilities beyond the narrow bounds of self and family. Creative policy can serve the common good, in a local school or on the other side of the world. John Buchan considered politics the "crown of a career" and a "most honorable adventure."[4] This has been our experience. Other young men and women will also find it so.

They must remember, however, that while politics is our duty, it is not our hope. It is a noble calling; it is not our ultimate destination. Christians are useful in public life precisely because they recognize a wide world of eternal values and meaning beyond the political realm. We work for the good and health of this earthly city. We hope for a city where there is no more death, no more tears, no more suffering, and no more sorrow.

"For we know," St. Paul wrote in his letter to the Corinthians, "that if the tent that is our earthly home is destroyed, we have a building from God, a house not made with hands, eternal in the heavens" (ESV). The City of Man is our residence for now, and we care for its order and justice. The City of God is our home.

NOTES

1. C. S. Lewis, *Letters of C. S. Lewis*, ed. W. H. Lewis and Walter Hooper (San Diego: Harcourt Brace, 1993), 414.

2. Sheldon Vanauken, *A Severe Mercy* (New York: HarperCollins, 1987), 234.

3. John Perkins, *Let Justice Roll Down* (Glendale, CA: G/L Regal Books, 1976), 103.

4. John Buchan, *Pilgrim's Way: An Autobiography* (New York: Carroll & Graf Publishers, 1984, reprint of the 1940 ed. published by Houghton Mifflin), 232.

Acknowledgments

A book is always the product of individuals beyond the authors, and *City of Man* is no exception.

We are grateful to Charles "Andy" Anderson, M. Craig Barnes, Karel Coppock, Martin Marty, and C. John Steer for their careful review of and comments on the section in the book dealing with the history of Christianity and politics. John Green provided extremely useful insights on the changes that are occurring within the evangelical movement. Adam Keiper offered typically thoughtful comments on the meaning of justice. And Michael Cromartie allowed us to benefit from his storehouse of knowledge, to say nothing of his impressive collection of books.

We want to pay particular tribute to Yuval Levin, a trusted colleague and friend who assisted us every step of the way—from the title of the book to the key arguments it ought to make. We greatly benefited from conversations with him and comments from him.

The Ethics and Public Policy Center, under the outstanding leadership of Ed Whelan, is an exemplary institution, one that cares about ideas and ideals, and it has been my (Peter Wehner) good fortune to call it my professional home for the second time in my career. It also provided a temporary home to Brian Weissenberg, a student at the University of California–Berkeley who interned at the Ethics and Public Policy Center and did outstanding work on everything from research to endnotes. Anna Carrington of the Institute for Global Engagement provided valuable assistance as well.

Madison Trammel of Moody Publishers first approached us about doing this book and worked with us from beginning to end. He provided sound counsel and encouragement, and he was a delight to work with. So was Chris Reese, Moody's excellent editor whose careful work made this a better book.

And then there is Neal Kozodoy. The essayist Joseph Epstein once called Neal "the best in the business." We tend to think he understated the case. From 1966 until 2009 Neal devoted his life to editing *Commentary* magazine, helping to make it one of the finest journals of opinion in America. Facing the prospect of writing this book in a very short period of time, we asked Neal if he would assist us, even though he really didn't have the time. No matter. Neal agreed, and he worked his magic. A brilliant editor and a dear friend, we are indebted to him.

One of the privileges of our lives has been to work in the arena of governing and politics. One of the reasons we remain hopeful rather than cynical about both is because of our own life experiences. It has been our great good fortune to work for individuals who were mentors to us, including William Bennett, Dan Coats, Charles Colson, and President George W. Bush. They taught us many things over the years, most especially the role courage and convictions must play in public life. And each one of them has had their political lives shaped by their personal faith. Being in their company, watching them operate up close, has made us better people.

Cindy Wehner and Dawn Gerson are the kind of women the author of Proverbs had in mind when he penned the thirty-first chapter. We're grateful for that, and we're very grateful for them.

April 2015
Goodwill
Hopkins
20¢